Ussher Surname

Ireland: 1600s to 1900s

From Ireland Church Records of Baptism, Marriage and Death

Comprised of Roman Catholic and Church of Ireland Records

From Counties Carlow, Cork, Kerry and Dublin City

Compiled by **Donovan Hurst**

February 1, 2012

ISBN: 098513433X
ISBN-13: 978-0-9851343-3-4

Dedication

This work is dedicated to all of those that came before us and shaped our lives to make us the people that we are today.

Table of Contents

Introduction

This is a compilation of individuals who have the surname of Ussher that lived in the country of Ireland from the 1600s to the 1900s. I have placed each entry into one of four categories: Families, Individual Births/Baptisms, Individual Burials, and Individual Marriages. If a marriage entry primarily concerns an Individual Ussher who is female, then I have placed that entry under the category of Individual Marriages. If a marriage entry primarily concerns an Individual Ussher who is male, then I have placed that entry under the category of Families. Images of many of these listings are available at http://churchrecords.irishgenealogy.ie/churchrecords/.

To help guide the reader of this work, the format of this book is as follows:

- Main Family Entry (Husband and Wife) (Father and Mother)

  - Child of Main Family Entry, including Spouse(s) when available

    - Grandchild of Main Family Entry, including Spouse(s) when available

      - Great-Grandchild of Main Family Entry, including Spouse(s) when available

(Bolded Text) following any entry includes any additional information such as Residence(s), Occupation(s), Signature(s), etc. when available.

Hurst

Some of the fonts used in this work symbolizes Celtic writing. The traditional letters, numbers, and punctuation marks and their Celtic counterparts are as follows:

Traditional Letters (Uppercase & Lowercase)

A a B b C c D d E f G g H h I i J j K k L l M m N n O o P p Q q R r S s T t U u V v W w X x Y y Z z

Celtic Letters (Uppercase & Lowercase)

A a B b C c D ð E e F ꝼ G g H h I í J j K k L l M m

N n O o P p Q q R ʀ S s T t U u V ʋ W ꞷ X x Y ẏ Z z

Traditional Numbers

1 2 3 4 5 6 7 8 9 10

Celtic Numbers

1 2 3 4 5 6 7 8 9 10

Traditional Punctuation

. , : ' " & - ( )

Celtic Punctuation

. , : ' " & - ( )

Parish Churches
Cork & Ross
(Roman Catholic or RC)

Cork - South Parish and Cork - SS. Peter & Paul Parish.

Dublin (Church of Ireland)

Clondalkin Parish, Harrington Street Parish, Lucan Parish, Milltown Parish, Rathmines Parish, St. Andrew Parish, St. Anne Parish, St. Audoen Parish, St. Bride Parish, St. Catherine Parish, St. George Parish, St. James Parish, St. John Parish, St. Kevin Parish, St. Luke Parish, St. Mark Parish, St. Mary Parish, St. Michael Parish, St. Michan Parish, St. Nicholas Within Parish, St. Nicholas Without Parish, St. Patrick Parish, St. Paul Parish, St. Peter Parish, St. Stephen Parish, St. Thomas Parish, St. Werburgh Parish, and Taney Parish.

Dublin (Roman Catholic or RC)

Clondalkin Parish, Lucan Parish, SS. Michael & John Parish, St. Andrew Parish, St. Audoen Parish, St. Catherine Parish, St. James Parish, St. Joseph Parish, St. Mary, Haddington Road Parish, St. Mary, Pro Cathedral Parish, St. Michan Parish, and St. Nicholas Parish.

Kerry (Church of Ireland)

Kilnaughtin Parish

Kerry (Roman Catholic or RC)

Ballylongford Parish, Causeway Parish, Listowel Parish, Moyvane Parish, and Tralee Parish.

$\mathbb{F}$amilies

- Adam Ussher & Rebecca Ussher, bur. 10 Aug 1695 (Burial, **St. Michan Parish**)

  o Anne Ussher – bapt. 24 Feb 1678 (Baptism, **St. Michan Parish**)

  o William Ussher – bapt. 12 May 1680 (Baptism, **St. Michan Parish**)

  o Rebecca Ussher – bapt. 18 Apr 1682 (Baptism, **St. Michan Parish**)

  o John Ussher – bapt. 8 Sep 1687 (Baptism, **St. Michan Parish**), bur. 11 May 1688 (Burial, **St. Michan Parish**)

  o Frederick Ussher – bapt. 23 Nov 1689 (Baptism, **St. Michan Parish**)

  o Adam Ussher – bapt. 28 Mar 1691 (Baptism, **St. Michan Parish**)

  o Arthur Ussher – bapt. 4 Aug 1692 (Baptism, **St. Michan Parish**), bur. 4 Feb 1693 (Burial, **St. Michan Parish**)

  o Charles Ussher – bapt. 6 Feb 1693 (Baptism, **St. Michan Parish**)

Adam Ussher (father):

Occupation - Minister - February 24, 1678

May 12, 1680

April 18, 1682

November 23, 1689

February 6, 1693

Clerk - September 8, 1687

March 28, 1691

August 4, 1692

Adam Ussher's wife, Rebecca, and children, John and Arthur, were placed in the third vault on the left hand in the chancel after they died.

Hurst

- Arlenter Ussher, bur. 17 Jun 1675 (Burial, **St. John Parish**) & Unknown

    o William Ussher – bapt. 23 Aug 1642 (Baptism, **St. John Parish**)

    o Robert Ussher – bur. 24 Jul 1643 (Burial, **St. John Parish**)

- Arthur Ussher & Mary Ussher

    o Mary Ussher – bapt. 29 Dec 1751 (Baptism, **St. Mary Parish**)

- Augustine Ussher & Judith Flinn

    o Margaret Ussher – b. 1765, bapt. 12 Oct 1765 (Baptism, **St. Catherine Parish** (RC))

    o Patrick Ussher – b. 1768, bapt. 1 Apr 1768 (Baptism, **St. Catherine Parish** (RC))

    o Michael Ussher – bapt. 11 Nov 1769 (Baptism, **St. Catherine Parish** (RC))

- Barnabas (B a r n a b a s) Ussher & Hannah Ussher

    o Jane Ussher – bapt. 16 Feb 1800 (Baptism, **St. Mary Parish**) & John McEvoy – 8 Jul 1816 (Marriage,

    Lucan Parish (RC)) (Marriage, **St. Mary, Haddington Road Parish** (RC))

- Beverly Ussher & Mary Lysaght – 26 Mar 1733 (Marriage, **St. Peter Parish**)

Beverly Ussher (husband):

   Residence - Consistory Court - March 26, 1733

- Charles Ussher & Catherine Unknown

    o Charles Ussher – bapt. 30 Jan 1823 (Baptism, **St. Audoen Parish** (RC))

- Charles Ussher & Esther Conway

    o Charles Ussher – bapt. 19 May 1784 (Baptism, **St. Michan Parish** (RC))

- Charles Ussher & Isabel Unknown

    o Robert Ussher – b. 28 Aug 1868, bapt. 10 Sep 1868 (Baptism, **St. John Parish**)

Charles Ussher (father):

   Residence - Christ Church Cathedral - September 10, 1868

   Occupation - Clerk - September 10, 1868

Ussher Surname Ireland: 1600s to 1900s

- Charles Ussher & Mary Unknown

  o Catherine Ussher – bapt. 28 Nov 1731 (Baptism, **St. Audoen Parish**)

  o Barbara Ussher – bapt. 11 Jan 1736 (Baptism, **St. Audoen Parish**)

- Charles Ussher & Mary Ussher

  o Elizabeth Ussher – bapt. 15 Dec 1726 (Baptism, **St. Catherine Parish**)

  o John Ussher – bapt. 1 Mar 1737 (Baptism, **St. Catherine Parish**)

- Charles Robert Ussher & Unknown

  o Charles William Ussher & Abigail Denehey – 22 Dec 1884 (Marriage, **St. Andrew Parish**)

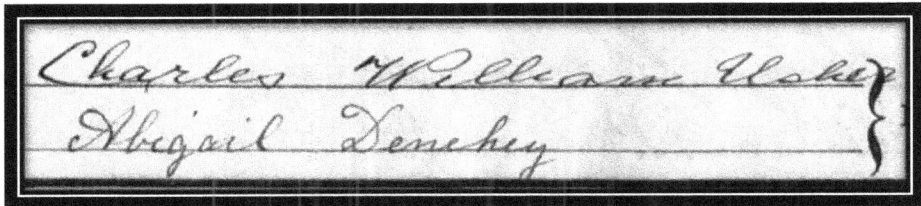

Signatures:

Charles William Ussher (son):

   Residence - HMS Belleisle Kingstown Harbor - December 22, 1884

   Occupation - Sailor - December 22, 1884

Abigail Denehey, daughter of Terence Denehey (daughter-in-law):

   Residence - 58 Dame Street - December 22, 1884

Terence Denehey (father):

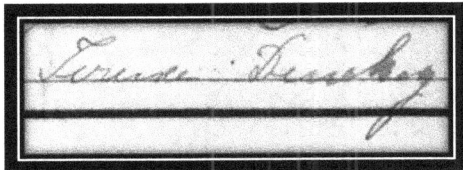

Signature:

   Occupation – Caretaker

Charles Robert Ussher (father):

   Occupation - Engine Fitter

Hurst

Wedding Witnesses:

John Evans & Terence Denehey

Signatures:

- Christopher Ussher, bur. 10 Jun 1706 (Burial, **St. Audoen Parish**) & Martha Ussher, bur. 31 Sep 1682 (Burial, **St. Audoen Parish**)
  - William Ussher – bapt. 16 Nov 1675 (Baptism, **St. Audoen Parish**)

Christopher Ussher (father):

Occupation - Esquire - November 16, 1675

June 10, 1706

- Christopher Musgrave Ussher & Unknown
  - Thomas O'Grady Ussher & Henrietta Mary Harris – 14 Jan 1869 (Marriage, **St. Stephen Parish**)

Signatures:

- Gertrude Elizabeth Ussher – b. 25 Oct 1867, bapt. 25 Nov 1867 (Baptism, **St. Stephen Parish**)
- Eleanor Melian Ussher – b. 5 Feb 1871, bapt. 7 Mar 1871 (Baptism, **St. Stephen Parish**)
- Thomas Harris Ussher – b. 30 Sep 1877, bapt. 22 Oct 1877 (Baptism, **St. Stephen Parish**)

Ussher Surname Ireland: 1600s to 1900s

Thomas O'Grady Ussher, son of Christopher Musgrave Ussher (son):

    Residence - Camphire Cappoquin - November 25, 1867

        Camphire Villierstown, Co. Waterford - January 14, 1869

        Camphire, Co. Waterford - March 7, 1871

      54 Fitzwilliam Square - October 22, 1877

    Occupation - Esquire - November 25, 1867

        January 14, 1869

        March 7, 1871

        October 22, 1877

Henrietta Mary Harris, daughter of Thomas Harris (daughter-in-law):

    Residence - 54 Fitzwilliam Square - January 14, 1869

Thomas Harris (father):

    Occupation - Barrister at Law

Christopher Musgrave Ussher (father):

    Occupation - Esquire

Wedding Witnesses:

Thomas Harris & A. E. Ussher

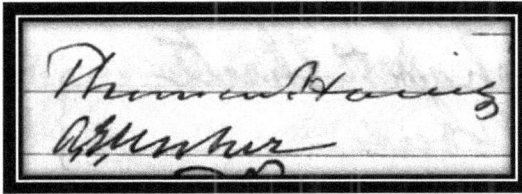

Signatures:

- Demess Ussher & Unknown

    o Jane Ussher – bur. 18 Oct 1703 (Burial, St. Audoen Parish)

- Dominick Ussher & Eleanor Sheridan – 4 Feb 1747 (Marriage, St. Catherine Parish (RC))

    o Dominick Ussher – bapt. 21 Jan 1750 (Baptism, St. Nicholas Parish (RC))

    o Gulielmo Ussher – bapt. 1750 (Baptism, St. Andrew Parish (RC))

    o Gulielmo Ussher – bapt. 1751 (Baptism, St. Andrew Parish (RC))

Hurst

- Dominick Ussher & Elizabeth Vaughn

  - Eleanor Ussher – bapt. 12 Mar 1780 (Baptism, **St. Nicholas Parish** (RC))

  - Anne Ussher – bapt. 29 Sep 1783 (Baptism, **St. Nicholas Parish** (RC))

  - Dominick Ussher – bapt. 11 Oct 1789 (Baptism, **St. Catherine Parish** (RC))

- Dominick Ussher & Mary Unknown

  - Gulielmo Ussher – bapt. 6 Oct 1742 (Baptism, **St. Nicholas Parish** (RC))

- Edward Ussher & Catherine Delloghery – 3 Oct 1857 (Marriage, **Causeway Parish** (RC))

  - Bridget Ussher – b. 22 Feb 1864, bapt. 24 Feb 1864 (Baptism, **Causeway Parish** (RC))

  - Catherine Ussher – b. 7 Apr 1872, bapt. 7 Apr 1872 (Baptism, **Causeway Parish** (RC))

Edward Ussher (father):

Residence - Kilmore - October 3, 1857

April 7, 1872

Ballyduff - February 24, 1864

- Edward Ussher & Catherine Keane

  - Thomas Ussher – b. 6 Dec 1858, bapt. 6 Dec 1858 (Baptism, **Causeway Parish** (RC))

  - Mary Ussher – b. 16 Oct 1861, bapt. 16 Oct 1861 (Baptism, **Causeway Parish** (RC))

  - John Ussher – b. 17 May 1866, bapt. 20 May 1866 (Baptism, **Causeway Parish** (RC))

  - Unknown Ussher – b. 12 Aug 1868, bapt. 18 Aug 1868 (Baptism, **Causeway Parish** (RC))

  - Elizabeth Ussher – b. 3 Jun 1870, bapt. 5 Jun 1870 (Baptism, **Causeway Parish** (RC))

Edward Ussher (father):

Residence - Kilmore - December 6, 1858

October 16, 1861

May 20, 1866

August 18, 1868

Knoppogue - June 5, 1870

Ussher Surname Ireland: 1600s to 1900s

- Edward Ussher & Jane Ussher

  o John Ussher – bapt. 21 Oct 1727 (Baptism, **St. Catherine Parish**)

- Evin Ussher and Unknown

  o Jane Ussher Moore & James McCullagh – 6 Dec 1864 (Marriage, **Clontarf Parish**)

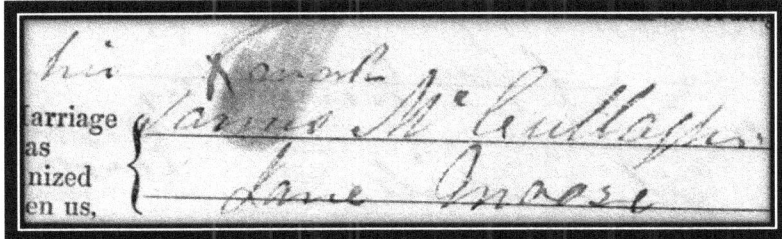

Signatures:

Jane Ussher (daughter):

  Residence - Albridge, The Sheds of Clontarf - December 6, 1864

  Relationship Status at Marriage - widow

James McCullagh, son of George McCullagh (son-in-law):

  Residence - Albridge, The Sheds of Clontarf - December 6, 1864

  Occupation -Laborer - December 6, 1864

George McCullagh (father):

  Occupation - Laborer

Evin Ussher (father):

  Occupation - Groom

- Francis Ussher & Anne Unknown

  o Margaret Ussher – bapt. 1795 (Baptism, **St. Andrew Parish (RC)**)

- Francis Ussher & Anne Unknown

  o Mary Ussher – bapt. 25 May 1803 (Baptism, **St. Paul Parish**)

  o William Ussher – bapt. 15 May 1805 (Baptism, **St. Paul Parish**)

  o Noble Luke Ussher – bapt. 11 Nov 1814 (Baptism, **St. Paul Parish**)

Hurst

- Francis Ussher & Anne Unknown

    o Eleanor Ussher – bapt. 14 Oct 1808 (Baptism, **St. Catherine Parish**)

Francis Ussher (father):

   Residence - Love Lane - October 14, 1808

- Francis Ussher & Mary Robinson – 24 Jun 1831 (Marriage, **St. Peter Parish**)

Francis Ussher (husband):

   Residence - Terrilspass, Co. Gifford Meath - June 24, 1831

Wedding Witnesses:

   John Ussher & John Crother

- Francis Ussher & Unknown

    o Anne Julie Ussher & Richard George Bushby, b. 1828 – 12 Aug 1852 (Marriage, **Lucan Parish**)

Anne Julie Ussher (daughter):

   Residence - Lucan Globe, Lucan - August 12, 1852

Richard George Bushby, son of William Peatt Bushby (son-in-law):

   Residence - Grove Park, Liverpool - August 12, 1852

William Peatt Bushby (father):

   Occupation - Esquire

Francis Ussher (father):

   Occupation - Esquire

Wedding Witnesses:

John Ussher & John M. A. Bushby

- Francis James Ussher & Mary Hardy

    o Verna Irene Ussher – b. 1 Jul 1893, bapt. 17 Sep 1893 (Baptism, **St. Kevin Parish**)

Francis James Ussher (father):

   Residence - Dolphin Villa South Circular Road - September 17, 1893

   Occupation - Merchant - September 17, 1893

Ussher Surname Ireland: 1600s to 1900s

- George Ussher & Anne Malpas – 14 Dec 1745 (Marriage, **St. Michan Parish (RC)**)

  - John Ussher – bapt. 1 Nov 1746 (Baptism, **St. Michan Parish (RC)**)

  - Christopher Ussher – bapt. 3 Jan 1750 (Baptism, **St. Michan Parish (RC)**)

- George Ussher & Jane Ussher

  - Maud Ussher – b. 8 Apr 1892, bapt. 20 Jun 1892 (Baptism, **St. Mark Parish**)

George Ussher (father):
Residence - 2 Coloins Terrace - June 20, 1892

- Gulielmo Ussher & Jane Lee – 30 May 1847 (Marriage, **St. Nicholas Parish (RC)**)

- Gulielmo Ussher & Jane Martin – 11 Jun 1824 (Marriage, **St. Nicholas Parish (RC)**)

  - Catherine Ussher – bapt. Jan 1823 (Baptism, **St. Nicholas Parish (RC)**)

- Gulielmo Ussher & Mary Kelly – Jul 1848 (Marriage, **St. Michan Parish (RC)**)

- Hemsworth Ussher & Elizabeth Derham – 5 Jul 1832 (Marriage, **St. Catherine Parish (RC)**)

  - Mary Jane Ussher – bapt. 30 Jul 1834 (Baptism, **St. Audoen Parish (RC)**)

- Henry Ussher & Barbara Unknown

  - Josaline Ussher – bapt. 18 Sep 1709 (Baptism, **St. Catherine Parish**)

  - Barbara Ussher – bapt. 23 Mar 1713 (Baptism, **St. Catherine Parish**)

  - Mason Ussher – bapt. 23 Mar 1713 (Baptism, **St. Catherine Parish**)

Hurst

- Henry Ussher & Judith Delahunty

  o Daniel Ussher & Anne Moorhouse Beneley – 31 May 1857 (Marriage, **St. Catherine Parish** (RC))

Daniel Ussher (son):

    Residence - Richmond Barracks - May 31, 1857

Anne Moorhouse Beneley, daughter of Charles Moorhouse & Dorothea Kelly

(daughter-in-law):

    Residence - 47 Coombe - May 31, 1857

    Relationship Status at Marriage - widow

Charles Moorhouse (father):

    Residence - 47 Coombe - May 31, 1857

Henry Ussher (father):

    Residence - 5 Circular Road - May 31, 1857

- Henry Ussher & Mary Ussher

  o William Ussher – b. 25 Jan 1855, bapt. 25 Feb 1855 (Baptism, **Kilnaughtin Parish**)

  o Mary Ussher – b. 4 Apr 1857, bapt. 5 Apr 1857 (Baptism, **Kilnaughtin Parish**)

Henry Ussher (father):

    Occupation - Policeman - February 25, 1855

- Henry Ussher & Sarah Marshall – 13 Feb 1733 (Marriage, **St. Michan Parish**)

Henry Ussher (husband):

    Occupation - Merchant - February 13, 1733

- Henry Ussher & Unknown – 7 Sep 1839 (Marriage, **St. Anne Parish**)

Ussher Surname Ireland: 1600s to 1900s

- Henry John Ussher & Sarah Ussher

  o Sarah Ussher – bapt. 26 Jul 1719 (Baptism, St. Mary Parish), bur. 4 Jul 1720 (Burial, St. Mary Parish)

  o Grace Ussher – b. 3 Dec 1724, bapt. 4 Dec 1724 (Baptism, St. Mary Parish), bur. 20 Dec 1724 (Burial, St. Mary Parish)

  o Anne Ussher – b. 6 Aug 1729, bapt. 27 Aug 1729 (Baptism, St. Mary Parish)

  o Christopher Ussher – b. 15 Aug 1730, bapt. 8 Sep 1730 (Baptism, St. Mary Parish)

  o Samuel Ussher – bapt. 13 Apr 1733 (Baptism, St. Mary Parish)

  o Thomas Ussher – bapt. 13 Feb 1734 (Baptism, St. Mary Parish)

- Isaac Ussher & Frances Parker – 1 May 1833 (Marriage, St. Mary Parish)

Signatures:

Isaac Ussher (husband);

   Residence - Donnybrook - May 1, 1833

Frances Parker (wife):

   Residence - St. Mary Parish - May 1, 1833

Wedding Witness:

Thomas Parker

Signature:

Hurst

- Isaac Ussher & Unknown

  - Isaac William Ussher & Rose Cecelia Alice Meyler – 6 Jul 1895 (Marriage, **Taney Parish**)

    - Isaac William Ussher – b. 14 May 1896, bapt. 24 Jun 1896 (Baptism, **Taney Parish**)

    - Rose Pricilla Emma May Ussher – b. 1 May 1898, bapt. 6 May 1898 (Baptism, **Taney Parish**)

    - Bloomfield Meyler Ussher – b. 12 Sep 1899, bapt. 16 Sep 1899 (Baptism, **Taney Parish**)

Isaac William Ussher (son):

    Residence - Tudor House, Dundrum - July 6, 1895

        Laurel Lodge, Dundrum - June 24, 1896

                May 6, 1898

                September 16, 1899

    Occupation - Medical Doctor - July 6, 1895

        Surgeon M D - June 24, 1896

             May 6, 1898

             September 16, 1899

Rose Cecelia Alice Meyler, daughter of George Meyler (daughter-in-law):

    Residence - Laurel Lodge - July 6, 1895

George Meyler (father):

    Occupation - Captain

Isaac Ussher (father):

    Occupation - Civil Service

- James Ussher & Bridget Walsh – 24 Oct 1742 (Marriage, **St. Michan Parish (RC)**)

- James Ussher & Catherine Holbrook

  - James Ussher – bapt. 11 Nov 1821 (Baptism, **SS. Michael & John Parish (RC)**)

Ussher Surname Ireland: 1600s to 1900s

- James Ussher & Eleanor Austin

  - Margaret Ussher – bapt. 4 Apr 1784 (Baptism, **St. Catherine Parish** (RC))

  - Anne Ussher – bapt. 21 Feb 1787 (Baptism, **St. Catherine Parish** (RC))

  - Catherine Ussher – bapt. 11 May 1788 (Baptism, **St. Catherine Parish** (RC))

  - John Ussher – bapt. 8 Apr 1790 (Baptism, **St. Catherine Parish** (RC))

  - Mary Ussher – bapt. 8 Apr 1790 (Baptism, **St. Catherine Parish** (RC))

  - Arthur Ussher – bapt. 3 May 1793 (Baptism, **St. Catherine Parish** (RC))

- James Ussher & Jane Firth – 27 May 1727 (Marriage, **St. Michan Parish**)

James Ussher (husband):

Occupation - Servant - May 27, 1727

- James Ussher & Margaret Boylan

  - Patrick Ussher – bapt. 16 Apr 1833 (Baptism, **St. Michan Parish** (RC))

  - Matthew Ussher – bapt. 16 May 1834 (Baptism, **St. Michan Parish** (RC))

  - Michael Ussher – bapt. Sep 1843 (Baptism, **St. Michan Parish** (RC))

  - Joseph Ussher – bapt. 13 Apr 1846 (Baptism, **St. Michan Parish** (RC))

- James Ussher & Margaret Unknown

  - John Ussher – bapt. 1824 (Baptism, **St. Andrew Parish** (RC))

- James Ussher & Margaret Unknown

  - Margaret Ussher – bapt. 19 Apr 1839 (Baptism, **St. Mary, Pro Cathedral Parish** (RC))

Hurst

- James Ussher, d. Before 18 Oct 1863, & Margaret Unknown

  - Julia Ussher & Edward McCormack (M c C o r m a c k)

    - Julia McCormack – b. 18 Jun 1875, Bapt. 18 Jun 1875 (Baptism, **St. Michan Parish** (RC))

Edward McCormack (father):

Residence - 26 Church Street - June 18, 1875

  - Michael Ussher & Sarah Murtagh – 18 Oct 1863 (Marriage, **St. Michan Parish** (RC))

    - Joseph Ussher – b. 4 Oct 1864, bapt. 14 Oct 1864 (Baptism, **St. Michan Parish** (RC))

    - William Ussher – b. 6 Jul 1866, bapt. 9 Jul 1866 (Baptism, **St. Michan Parish** (RC))

    - Mary Margaret Ussher – b. 4 Dec 1868, bapt. 7 Dec 1868 (Baptism, **St. Michan Parish** (RC))

    - Patrick Joseph Ussher – b. 12 Mar 1871, bapt. 20 Mar 1871 (Baptism, **St. Michan Parish** (RC))

    - Mary Anne Ussher – b. 17 Jun 1873, bapt. 20 Jun 1873 (Baptism, **St. Michan Parish** (RC))

    - James Ussher – b. 31 Jan 1876, bapt. 7 Feb 1876 (Baptism, **St. Michan Parish** (RC))

    - Bridget Ussher – b. 26 Jan 1878, bapt. 30 Jan 1878 (Baptism, **St. Michan Parish** (RC))

    - Augustine Ussher – b. 26 Aug 1882, bapt. 28 Aug 1882 (Baptism, **St. Michan Parish** (RC))

Michael Ussher (son):

Residence - 26 Church Street - October 18, 1863

October 14, 1864

July 9, 1866

December 7, 1868

March 20, 1871

June 20, 1873

February 7, 1876

27 Church Street - January 30, 1878

9 Anne Street - August 28, 1882

Sarah Murtagh, daughter of Gulielmo Murtagh & Catherine Unknown (daughter-in-law):

Residence - 26 Church Street - October 18, 1863

Ussher Surname Ireland: 1600s to 1900s

Gulielmo Murtagh (father):

Residence - 26 Church Street - October 18, 1863

Margaret Unknown (mother):

Residence - 38 Church Street - October 18, 1863

- James Ussher & Mary Donnelly

  o Mary Frances Ussher – bapt. 16 Dec 1840 (Baptism, **St. Nicholas Parish (RC)**)

- James Ussher & Mary Fitcock

  o James Ussher – bapt. 14 Jul 1828 (Baptism, **St. Nicholas Parish (RC)**)

- James Ussher & Mary Ussher

  o James Ussher – b. 2 Apr 1816, bapt. 3 Apr 1816 (Baptism, **St. Werburgh Parish**)

James Ussher (father):

Residence - Cork Street - April 3, 1816

- James Ussher & Mary Sarah Leonard

  o Sarah Ussher – b. 1870, bapt. 1870 (Baptism, **Clondalkin Parish (RC)**)

  o John Joseph Ussher – b. 1874, bapt. 1874 (Baptism, **Clondalkin Parish (RC)**)

James Ussher (father):

Residence - Colblow - 1870

Lucan - 1874

Hurst

- James Ussher & Unknown

  - Teresa Ussher & Samuel Sleater – 14 May 1850 (Marriage, **St. Paul Parish**)

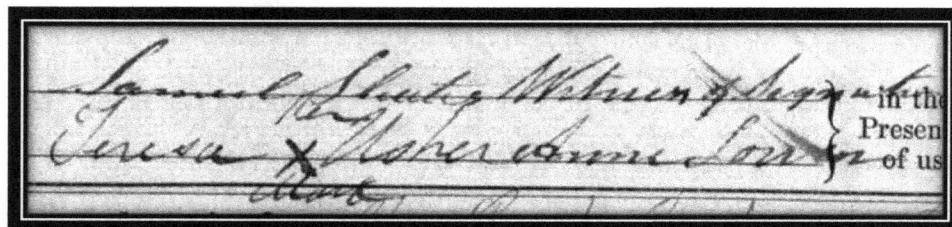

Signatures:

Teresa Ussher (daughter):

Residence - Tighe Street - May 14, 1850

Occupation - Servant - May 14, 1850

Samuel Sleater, son of James Sleater (son-in-law):

Residence - Royal Barracks - May 14, 1850

Occupation - Private in the 9th Regiment - May 14, 1850

James Sleater (father):

Occupation - Sexton

James Ussher (father):

Occupation - School Master

- James Charles Neville Ussher & Mary Hitchcock – 27 Mar 1842 (Marriage, **St. Nicholas Parish** (RC))

  - Frances Caroline Neville Ussher, bapt. 24 Nov 1843 (Baptism, **St. Nicholas Parish** (RC)) & William

    Thomas Cummins – 26 Jul 1882 (Marriage, **St. Peter Parish**)

Frances Caroline Neville Ussher (daughter):

Residence - 19 A St. Albans Road South Circular Road - July 26, 1882

William Thomas Cummins, son of William Cummins (son-in-law):

Residence - 6 Camden Row - July 26, 1882

Occupation - Army Relief Corps - July 26, 1882

Ussher Surname Ireland: 1600s to 1900s

William Cummins (father):

  Occupation - Gun Maker

James Charles Neville Ussher (father):

  Occupation - Classical Teacher

- Jason Ussher & Margaret Keating

  o James Ussher – bapt. 14 Feb 1773 (Baptism, **St. Catherine Parish (RC)**)

- John Ussher & Alice Unknown

  o Silvestor Ussher – bur. 11 Oct 1672 (Burial, **St. Audoen Parish**)

- John Ussher, bur. 5 Jun 1688 (Burial, **St. Michan Parish**) & Alice Unknown, bur. 21 May 1688 (Burial,

  St. Michan Parish)

  o John Ussher – bur. 20 Dec 1672 (Burial, **St. Michan Parish**)

John Ussher (father):

  Social Status - Yeoman - December 20, 1672

- John Ussher & Alice Unknown

  o William Ussher – bapt. 15 Apr 1683 (Baptism, **St. Catherine Parish**)

  o Samuel Ussher – bapt. 16 Jul 1684 (Baptism, **St. Catherine Parish**)

  o Christopher Ussher – b. 13 Jan 1686, bapt. Unclear (Baptism, **St. Catherine Parish**)

  o Mary Ussher – bapt. 8 Sep 1690 (Baptism, **St. Catherine Parish**)

  o Judith Ussher – bapt. 17 Oct 1691 (Baptism, **St. Catherine Parish**)

- John Ussher, bur. 26 Feb 1732 (Burial, **St. Audoen Parish**) & Alice Unknown, bur. 30 Nov 1709 (Burial,

  St. Audoen Parish)

  o Alice Ussher – bur. 7 Apr 1707 (Burial, **St. Audoen Parish**)

John Ussher (father):

  Professional Title - Dr.

Hurst

- John Ussher & Alice Ussher

  - Jane Ussher – bapt. 17 Feb 1693 (Baptism, **St. Michan Parish**)

  - William Ussher – bapt. 24 Jul 1697 (Baptism, **St. Michan Parish**)

John Ussher (father):

Occupation - Esquire Council at Laws - February 17, 1693

July 24, 1697

- John Ussher & Amelia Reilly – 4 May 1788 (Marriage, **St. Michan Parish**)

John Ussher (husband):

Residence - City of Dublin - May 4, 1788

Occupation - Servant - May 4, 1788

Amelia Reilly (wife):

Residence - St. Michan's Parish - May 4, 1788

- John Ussher & Anne Driscol – 30 May 1801 (Marriage, **St. Andrew Parish (RC)**)

- John Ussher & Anne Unknown

  - Joshua Ussher – bapt. 15 Feb 1756 (Baptism, **St. Nicholas Without Parish**)

  - Jane Ussher – bapt. 12 Jun 1757 (Baptism, **St. Nicholas Without Parish**)

John Ussher (father):

Residence - Frans Street - February 15, 1756

June 12, 1757

- John Ussher & Anne Ussher

  - John Ussher – bapt. 25 Feb 1754 (Baptism, **St. Audoen Parish**)

- John Ussher & Bridget Unknown

  - Eleanor Ussher – bapt. 11 Feb 1745 (Baptism, **St. Mary, Pro Cathedral Parish (RC)**)

- John Ussher & Catherine Unknown

  - Barbara Ussher – bapt. 7 Apr 1749 (Baptism, **St. Michan Parish (RC)**)

- John Ussher & Elizabeth Dickison – 21 Jul 1764 (Marriage, **St. Andrew Parish**)

Ussher Surname Ireland: 1600s to 1900s

- John Ussher & Elizabeth Unknown

  o Thomas Ussher – bapt. 8 May 1757 (Baptism, **St. Catherine Parish**)

- John Ussher & Elizabeth Ussher

  o Hannah Ussher – bapt. 2 Jan 1738 (Baptism, **St. Audoen Parish**)

- John Ussher & Frances Unknown

  o John Ussher – bapt. 12 Mar 1821 (Baptism, **St. Mary, Pro Cathedral Parish (RC)**)

John Ussher (father):

Residence - 5 Phoenix Street - March 12, 1821

- John Ussher & Jane Ussher

  o Jane Ussher – bapt. 18 Sep 1720 (Baptism, **St. Catherine Parish**)

- John Ussher & Mary Unknown

  o Bridget Ussher – bapt. 11 Jan 1748 (Baptism, **St. Michan Parish (RC)**)

- John Ussher & Mary Unknown

  o Sophia Ussher – bapt. 22 Oct 1771 (Baptism, **St. Werburgh Parish**)

John Ussher (father):

Residence - George's Lane - October 22, 1771

- John Ussher & Mary Unknown

  o Michael Frederick Ussher – bapt. 10 Sep 1834 (Baptism, **SS. Michael & John Parish (RC)**)

  o Sarah Ussher – bapt. 27 Jun 1838 (Baptism, **SS. Michael & John Parish (RC)**)

  o Mary Ussher – bapt. May 1841 (Baptism, **SS. Michael & John Parish (RC)**)

  o Margaret Ussher – bapt. 14 Dec 1843 (Baptism, **SS. Michael & John Parish (RC)**)

  o Josh Francis Ussher – bapt. Feb 1846 (Baptism, **SS. Michael & John Parish (RC)**)

Hurst

- John Ussher & Mary Unknown

    - John Ussher – bapt. 1837 (Baptism, **St. Andrew Parish** (RC))

    - Mary Casey Ussher – bapt. 1840 (Baptism, **St. Andrew Parish** (RC))

- John Ussher & Mary Unknown

    - Lucy Ussher – bapt. 24 Apr 1842 (Baptism, **St. Mary, Pro Cathedral Parish** (RC))

    - Mary Ussher – bapt. 10 Sep 1844 (Baptism, **St. Mary, Pro Cathedral Parish** (RC))

    - Thomas Ussher –bapt. 9 May 1848 (Baptism, **St. Mary, Pro Cathedral Parish** (RC))

- John Ussher & Mary Ussher

    - Mary Ussher – bapt. 18 Oct 1737 (Baptism, **St. Catherine Parish**)

- John Ussher & Mary Ussher

    - John Wilson Ussher – b. 20 Sep 1837, bapt. 24 Sep 1837 (Baptism, **St. Mark Parish**)

John Ussher (father):

Residence - 128 Townsend Street - September 24, 1837

Occupation - Seaman - September 24, 1837

- John Ussher & Mary Ussher

    - William Ussher – b. 25 Jun 1844, bapt. 22 Sep 1844 (Baptism, **St. Catherine Parish**)

    - Adelaide Elizabeth Ussher – b. 21 Feb 1850, bapt. 7 Mar 1850 (Baptism, **St. Mary Parish**)

    - Olivia Rosanna Ussher – b. 21 Feb 1850, bapt. 7 Mar 1850 (Baptism, **St. Mary Parish**)

John Ussher (father):

Residence - 69 Cork Street - September 22, 1844

25 Mary's Abbey - March 7, 1850

Occupation - Tailor - September 22, 1844

March 7, 1850

Ussher Surname Ireland: 1600s to 1900s

- John Ussher & Mary Ussher

  - Elizabeth Love Ussher – b. 15 Jun 1858, bapt. 13 May 1859 (Baptism, **St. Mark Parish**)

  - John George Ussher – b. 3 Sep 1860, bapt. 9 Nov 1860 (Baptism, **St. Mark Parish**)

  - Thomas Albert Bismarck Ussher – b. 2 Jan 1872, bapt. 18 Jul 1873 (Baptism, **St. Mark Parish**)

John Ussher (father):

Residence - 7 Mark Street - May 13, 1859

    16 South Cumberland Street - November 9, 1860

   17 Luke Street - July 18, 1873

Occupation - Scripture Reader - May 13, 1859

      November 9, 1860

   Lay Missionary - July 18, 1873

- John Ussher & Sarah Ussher

  - Joseph Ussher – bur. 15 Nov 1731 (Burial, **St. Mary Parish**)

  - John Ussher – bur. 18 Jul 1732 (Burial, **St. Mary Parish**)

- John Ussher & Sarah Ussher

  - Alice Ussher – bapt. 26 Mar 1735 (Baptism, **St. Audoen Parish**)

  - George Ussher – bapt. 26 Mar 1735 (Baptism, **St. Audoen Parish**)

  - John Ussher – bapt. 20 Apr 1736 (Baptism, **St. Audoen Parish**)

- John Ussher & Unknown

  - Richard Ussher – bur. 2 Feb 1668 (Burial, **St. Michan Parish**)

John Ussher (father):

Occupation - Car Man - February 2, 1668

- John Ussher & Unknown

  o William Ussher – bur. 30 Mar 1684 (Burial, **St. Audoen Parish**)

  o Samuel Ussher – bur. 28 Jan 1687 (Burial, **St. Audoen Parish**)

  o Martha Ussher – bur. 21 Jan 1692 (Burial, **St. Audoen Parish**)

  o Mary Ussher – bur. 9 Oct 1697 (Burial, **St. Audoen Parish**)

John Ussher (father):

Occupation - Counselor - March 30, 1684

January 28, 1687

Esquire - October 9, 1697

- John Ussher, b. 1729, bur. 29 Jan 1829 (Burial, **Clontarf Parish**) & Unknown

  o John Ussher, b. 1766, bur. 15 Jul 1823 (Burial, **Clontarf Parish**)

    ▪ Jane Georgiana Ussher & Charles Henry Leet – 4 Jul 1828 (Marriage, **Clontarf Parish**)

Jane Georgiana Ussher (wife):

Residence - Clontarf - July 4, 1828

Charles Henry Leet (husband):

Residence - St. Peter's Parish - July 4, 1828

Occupation - Esquire - July 4, 1828

Wedding Witnesses:

And Leet & R. B. Ussher

    ▪ John Ussher & Margaret Connor – 22 Feb 1837 (Marriage, **St. George Parish**)

Signatures:

Ussher Surname Ireland: 1600s to 1900s

- John George Ussher – b. 3 Sep 1838, bapt. 26 Sep 1838 (Baptism, **St. George Parish**)

- Thomas Connor Ussher – b. 19 Jun 1842, bapt. 15 Jul 1842 (Baptism, **St. George Parish**)

- James Henry Ussher – b. 1 Nov 1844, bapt. 27 Nov 1844 (Baptism, **St. George Parish**)

- Charles Edward Ussher – b. 2 Jul 1847, bapt. 11 Aug 1847 (Baptism, **St. George Parish**)

John Ussher (son):

Residence - No 2 Upper Rutland Street - February 22, 1837

September 26, 1838

No 28 Upper Temple Street - July 15, 1842

Elm Ville Harold's Cross - November 27, 1844

Elm Ville near Harold's Cross - August 11, 1847

Occupation - Captain Half pay Unattached - February 22, 1837

July 15, 1842

Captain on Half Pay in the Army - September 26, 1838

Esquire - July 15, 1842

Captain in the Army - November 27, 1844

Captain Late 50th Regiment Unattached - August 11, 1847

Margaret Connor, daughter of Unknown Connor (daughter-in-law):

Residence - 25 Upper Temple Street - February 22, 1837

Wedding Witnesses:

George (Unclear)ington Connor, R. B. Ussher, and C. H. Leet

Signatures:

Hurst

- Richard Beverly Ussher & Henrietta Jane Boileau – 3 Aug 1822 (Marriage, **St. Peter Parish**)

Signatures:

- John Theophilus Ussher – b. 4 Sep 1823, bapt. 16 Sep 1823 (Baptism, **Clontarf Parish**) &

  Annabella Ross – 2 Oct 1851 (Marriage, **St. Peter Parish**)

Signatures:

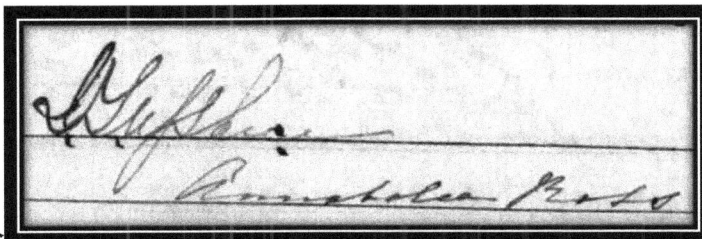

Signatures (Marriage):

1. Beverly William Reed Usshər – b. 4 Apr 1853, bapt. 1 May 1853 (Baptism, **St. Peter Parish**)

2. Allan Vesey Ussher – b. 13 Sep 1860, bapt. 22 Oct 1860 (Baptism, **St. Peter Parish**)

John Theophilus Ussher (son):

Residence - 60 Harcourt Street - October 2, 1851

May 1, 1853

Cavan, Co. Cavan - October 22, 1860

Occupation - Lieutenant 91st Regiment - October 2, 1851

Sergeant 91st Regiment - May 1, 1853

Captain Staff Office - October 22, 1860

Annabella Ross, daughter of Kenneth Tolmie Ross (daughter-in-law):

Residence -39 Leinster Road Rathmines - October 2, 1851

Kenneth Tolmie Ross (father):

Occupation - Paymaster 66th Regiment

Richard Beverly Ussher (father):

Occupation - Captain 86th Regiment

Hurst

Wedding Witnesses:

R. B. Ussher & William Ross

Signatures:

- Simeon Ussher & Mary Jane Morris – 23 Sep 1851 (Marriage, **St. Anne Parish**)

Signatures:

1. Richard Ussher – b. 30 Apr 1856, bapt. 29 May 1856 (Baptism, **St. James Parish**)

2. Robert Movies Ussher – b. 19 Mar 1859, bapt. 29 Apr 1859 (Baptism, **St. James Parish**)

3. Alena Jane Ussher & George Wyclif Yeates – 21 Nov 1888 (Marriage, **St. Stephen Parish**)

Signatures:

Alena Jane Ussher (daughter):

Residence - 46 Upper Leeson Street - November 21, 1888

George Wyclif Yeates, son of George Yeates (son-in-law):

Residence - 25 Lower Baggot Street - November 21, 1888

Occupation - Esquire M B - November 21, 1888

George Yeates (father):

Occupation - Clerk in Holy Orders

Simeon Ussher (father):

Occupation - Esquire

Wedding Witnesses:

R. A. Yeates & G. N. Ussher

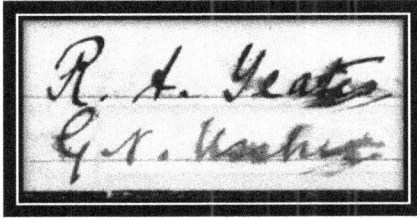

Signatures:

4. Henrietta Ussher, b. 29 Jul 1860, bapt. 23 Aug 1860 (Baptism, **St. James Parish**) & George William Place – 15 Oct 1885 (Marriage, **Leeson Park Parish**)

Henrietta Ussher (daughter):

Residence - 46 Upper Leeson Street - October 15, 1885

George William Place, son of Charles Godfrey Place (son-in-law):

Residence - 14 Clare Street - October 15, 1885

Occupation - Bengal Civil Service - October 15, 1885

Charles Godfrey Place (father):

Occupation - Bank of Ireland Agent

Simeon Ussher (father):

Occupation - Gentleman

Hurst

Wedding Witnesses:

John T. Ussher & Arthur H. Benson

Signatures:

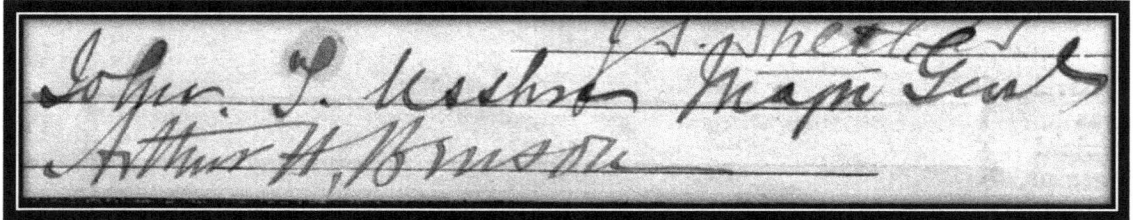

5. Anne Ussher – b. 27 Jan 1863, bapt. 5 Mar 1863 (Baptism, **St. James Parish**)

Simeon Ussher (son):

Residence - James Gate - September 23, 1851

103 James Street - May 29, 1856

81 James Street - April 29, 1859

August 23, 1860

March 5, 1863

Occupation - Brewer - September 23, 1851

May 29, 1856

April 29, 1859

August 23, 1860

March 5, 1863

Gentleman

Mary Jane Morris, daughter of Robert Morris (daughter-in-law):

Residence - 34 Dawson Street - September 23, 1851

Relationship Status at Marriage - minor age

Robert Morris (father):

Occupation - Solicitor

Richard Beverly Ussher (father):

Occupation - Druggist

Ussher Surname Ireland: 1600s to 1900s

Wedding Witnesses:

J. T. Ussher & Thomas Morris

Signatures:

- Beverly Ussher & Charlotte Emilia Smyth – 14 Sep 1852 (Marriage, **St. Peter Parish**)

Signatures:

1. George Neville Ussher – b. 21 Nov 1856, bapt. 1 Jan 1857 (Baptism, **St. Peter Parish**)

2. Charlotte Elizabeth Ussher – b. 9 Jun 1858, bapt. 25 Jul 1858 (Baptism, **St. Peter Parish**)

3. Emily Ussher – b. 24 Jan 1861, bapt. 17 Mar 1861 (Baptism, **St. Peter Parish**)

Beverly Ussher (son):

Residence - 60 Harcourt Street - September 14, 1852

13 Charlemont Place - January 1, 1857

July 25, 1858

Charlemont Place - March 17, 1861

Occupation - Esquire - September 14, 1852

July 25, 1858

March 17, 1861

Agent - January 1, 1857

Hurst

Charlotte Emily Smyth, daughter of Richard Smyth (daughter-in-law):

    Residence - 27 Harcourt Street - September 14, 1852

Richard Smyth (father):

    Occupation - Esquire

Richard Beverly Ussher (father):

    Occupation - Captain 86th Regiment

               Captain 87th Regiment

Wedding Witnesses:

George Smyth & R. B. Ussher

Signatures:

- Henry Ussher – b. 10 Jan 1833, bapt. 1833 (Baptism, **St. Peter Parish**)

- Peter Roe Clarke Ussher – b. 26 Mar 1834, bapt. 5 May 1834 (Baptism, **St. Peter Parish**)

- Jane Anne Ussher – b. 22 Nov 1835, bapt. 19 Jan 1836 (Baptism, **St. Peter Parish**)

- Isabel Madeline Ussher – b. 28 May 1837, bapt. 3 Aug 1837 (Baptism, **St. Peter Parish**)

- Henrietta Ussher – b. 3 Nov 1839, bapt. 20 Nov 1839 (Baptism, **St. Peter Parish**)

- James Ussher – b. 14 May 1842, bapt. 6 Jun 1842 (Baptism, **St. Catherine Parish**)

- Bromdum Boileau Ussher – b. 3 Aug 1845, bapt. 23 Aug 1845 (Baptism, **St. Catherine Parish**)

Ussher Surname Ireland: 1600s to 1900s

Richard Beverly Ussher (father):

    Residence - 16 Charlemont Place - January 10, 1833

                    May 5, 1834

                    January 19, 1836

          Pembroke Road - August 3, 1837

        5 Pembroke Road - November 20, 1839

        James Gate - June 6, 1842

                August 23, 1845

    Occupation - Lieutenant in the 86th Regiment - August 3, 1822

          Of the 86th Regiment - January 10, 1833

                  May 5, 1834

        Gentleman - August 23, 1845

        Captain 87th Regiment

        Druggist

Henrietta Jane Boileau, daughter of Unknown Boileau (daughter-in-law):

    Residence - St. Peter Parish - August 3, 1822

Wedding Witnesses:

Simon Boileau & George Boileau Wilson

John Ussher (son):

    Residence - Co. Dublin - July 15, 1823

    Occupation - M. D. - July 15, 1823

    Age at Death - 57 years

John Ussher (father):

    Occupation - Reverend

    Age at Death - 100 years

    Remarks - He has been a reverend of Clontarf Parish of which he has been an

        incumbent 52 yrs up to March 1811, when he resigned.

- John Ussher & Unknown

  - Daniel Ussher – bapt. 29 Jun 1740 (Baptism, St. Catherine Parish)

Hurst

- John Ussher & Unknown

  o John Xavirius Ussher & Isabel Anne Dillon – 21 Sep 1869 (Marriage, **St. Anne Parish**)

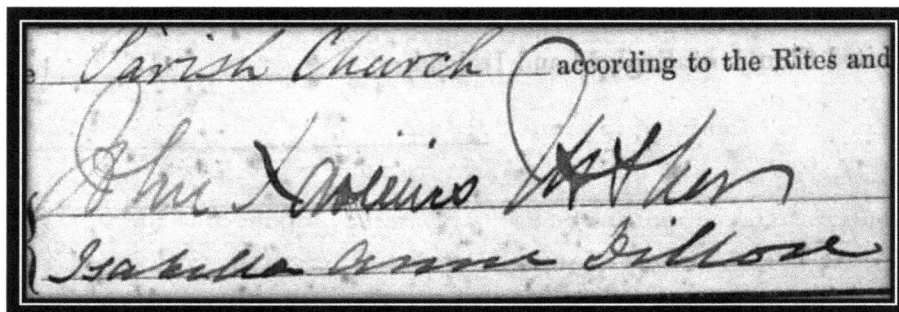

Signatures:

John Xavirius Ussher (son):

  Residence - Keavin Hotel Kildare Street - September 21, 1869

  Occupation - Gentleman - September 21, 1869

Isabel Anne Dillon, daughter of John Dillon (daughter-in-law):

  Residence - Kildare Street - September 21, 1869

John Dillon (father):

  Occupation - Captain 1st Royal Dragoon Guards

John Ussher (father):

  Occupation - Gentleman

- John Ussher & Unknown

  o Richard Ussher (1st Marriage) & Charlotte McTye Livingstone – 6 Jun 1850 (Marriage, **St. Peter Parish**)

Signatures:

Richard Ussher (son):

   Residence - White Church, New Ross - June 6, 1850

   Occupation - Esquire - June 6, 1850

Charlotte McTye Livingstone, daughter of James McTye (daughter-in-law):

   Residence - 42 Lower Mount Street - June 6, 1850

   Relationship Status at Marriage - widow

James McTye (father):

   Occupation - Clerk

John Ussher (father):

   Occupation - Esquire

o Richard Ussher (2nd Marriage) & Mary Carroll – 5 Aug 1876 (Marriage, **Rathmines Parish**)

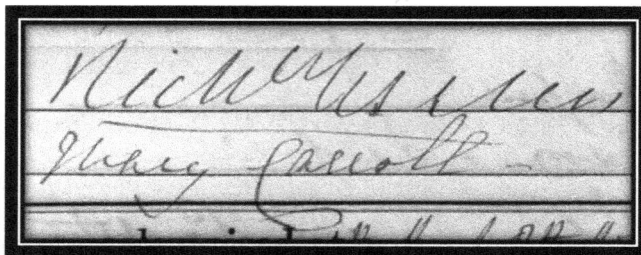

Signatures:

Richard Ussher (son):

    Residence - Landscape New Ross - August 5, 1876

    Occupation - Esquire - August 5. 1876

    Relationship Status at Marriage - widow

Mary Carroll, daughter of William Hales Carroll (daughter-in-law):

    Residence - 7 William's Park Rathmines - August 5, 1876

William Hales Carroll (father):

Signature:

    Occupation - Solicitor

John Ussher (father):

    Occupation - Esquire

Wedding Witnesses:

W. Hales Carroll & R. T. Wolfe

Signatures:

Ussher Surname Ireland: 1600s to 1900s

- John Ussher & Unknown Myler – 7 Jul 1802 (Marriage, **St. Andrew Parish**)

John Ussher (husband):

    Professional Title - Dr.

- John Ussher & Unknown Tighe – 27 Nov 1836 (Marriage, **St. Andrew Parish (RC)**)

- Josalan Ussher & Eleanor Ussher

  - Eleanor Ussher – b. 10 Aug 1714, bapt. 14 Aug 1714 (Baptism, **St. Mary Parish**)

  - Henry Ussher – b. 10 Aug 1714, bapt. 14 Aug 1714 (Baptism, **St. Mary Parish**)

Josalan Ussher (father):

    Occupation - Gentleman - August 14, 1714

- Joseph Ussher & Bridget Evans – 2 Mar 1851 (Marriage, **St. Andrew Parish (RC)**)

  - James Ussher – b. 1852, bapt. 1852 (Baptism, **St. Andrew Parish (RC)**)

  - Mary Bridget Ussher – b. 1854, bapt. 1854 (Baptism, **St. Andrew Parish (RC)**)

- Joseph Ussher & Bridget Unknown

  - Julia Ussher – bapt. 22 Apr 1836 (Baptism, **St. Mary, Pro Cathedral Parish (RC)**)

  - Esther Ussher – bapt. 25 Apr 1838 (Baptism, **St. Mary, Pro Cathedral Parish (RC)**)

- Joseph Ussher & Unknown – 16 Aug 1841 (Marriage, **St. Michan Parish (RC)**)

- Joseph Ussher & Unknown

  o Joseph Ussher & Rebecca Christian – 28 Apr 1857 (Marriage, **St. Peter Parish**)

Signatures:

Joseph Ussher (son):

  Residence - 8 Merrion Square North - April 28, 1857

  Occupation - Servant - April 28, 1857

Rebecca Christian, daughter of James Christian (daughter-in-law):

  Residence - Richmond Hall Clonskea - April 28, 1857

  Occupation - Servant - April 28, 1857

James Christian (father):

  Occupation - Farmer

Joseph Ussher (father):

  Occupation - Laborer

- Joseph Ussher & Unknown

  o William Egan Ussher & Matilda Hall – 9 Apr 1890 (Marriage, **St. Mary Parish**)

Signatures:

Ussher Surname Ireland: 1600s to 1900s

William Egan Ussher (son):

    Residence - 21 Glengariffe Parada South Circular Road - April 9, 1890

    Occupation - Commercial Clerk - April 9, 1890

Matilda Hall, daughter of George Hall (daughter-in-law):

    Residence - 6 Middle Mount Joy Street - April 9, 1890

George Hall (father):

    Occupation - Commercial Traveller

Joseph Ussher (father):

    Occupation - Gentleman

- Lawrence Ussher & Eleanor Ussher

  o William Ussher – bapt. 28 Feb 1732 (Baptism, **St. Catherine Parish**)

- Mark Charles Neville Ussher & Mary Dwyer – 22 May 1782 (Marriage, **Cork - South Parish (RC)**)

  o James Ussher – bapt. 3 Oct 1789 (Baptism, **Cork - South Parish (RC)**)

  o Michael Ussher – bapt. 3 Oct 1789 (Baptism, **Cork - South Parish (RC)**)

  o Gilbert James Neville Ussher – bapt. 23 May 1791 (Baptism, **Cork = South Parish (RC)**)

  o Frances Mary Ussher – bapt. 7 Jan 1794 (Baptism, **Cork - South Parish (RC)**)

  o Mary Teresa Ussher – bapt. 7 Jan 1794 (Baptism, **Cork - South Parish (RC)**)

Mark Charles Neville Ussher (father):

    Residence - Grand Parade - October 3, 1789

                    May 23, 1791

                    January 7, 1794

- Matthew Ussher & Elizabeth Smyth

  o John Ussher – b. 25 Nov 1879, bapt. Nov 1879 (Baptism, **St. Catherine Parish (RC)**)

Matthew Ussher (father):

    Residence - 61 Meath Street - Nov 1879

- Matthew Ussher & Mary Henry – 2 Dec 1732 (Marriage, **St. Michan Parish (RC)**)

Hurst

- Michael Ussher & Mary Wolfe – 8 Feb 1803 (Marriage, **St. Catherine Parish** (RC))

  - John Ussher – bapt. 23 Nov 1803 (Baptism, **St. Catherine Parish** (RC))

  - James Ussher – bapt. Mar 1813 (Baptism, **St. Nicholas Parish** (RC))

- Patrick Ussher & Bridget Unknown

  - Patrick Ussher & Mary Byrne (B y r n e) – 9 Oct 1875 (Marriage, **St. Andrew Parish** (RC))

    - Michael Ussher – b. 10 Jul 1876, bapt. 14 Jul 1876 (Baptism, **St. Michan Parish** (RC))

Patrick Ussher (son):

Residence - Monasterboice - October 9, 1875

49 Bolton Street - July 14, 1876

Mary Byrne, daughter of Michael Byrne & Anne Unknown (daughter-in-law):

Residence - 14 Cuffe Street - October 9, 1875

- Patrick Ussher & Eleanor Unknown

  - Michael Ussher – bapt. 19 Oct 1746 (Baptism, **St. Michan Parish** (RC))

  - Alice Ussher – bapt. 8 Nov 1747 (Baptism, **St. Michan Parish** (RC))

  - Eleanor Ussher – bapt. 26 Feb 1748 (Baptism, **St. Michan Parish** (RC))

  - Patrick Ussher – bapt. 10 Jun 1750 (Baptism, **St. Michan Parish** (RC))

- Patrick Ussher & Mary Murphy – 11 Aug 1842 (Marriage, **Cork - South Parish** (RC))

  - Mary Honora Ussher – bapt. 28 Dec 1845 (Baptism, **Cork - SS. Peter & Paul Parish** (RC))

- Patrick Ussher & Mary Unknown

  - William Ussher – bapt. 15 Nov 1745 (Baptism, **St. Michan Parish** (RC))

- Patrick Ussher & Mary Unknown

  - Eleanor Ussher – bapt. 26 Feb 1749 (Baptism, **St. Michan Parish** (RC))

Ussher Surname Ireland: 1600s to 1900s

- Peter Ussher & Anne Holland – 15 Apr 1733 (Marriage, **St. Mary Parish**)

  - James Ussher – bapt. 10 Dec 1737 (Baptism, **St. Werburgh Parish**)

  - Christopher Ussher – bapt. 12 Nov 1739 (Baptism, **St. Werburgh Parish**)

  - David Ussher – bapt. 26 Oct 1741 (Baptism, **St. Werburgh Parish**)

  - Margaret Ussher – bapt. Dec 1742 (Baptism, **St. Werburgh Parish**), bur. 20 Sep 1745 (Burial, **St. Werburgh Parish**)

  - Peter Ussher – bapt. 15 Jan 1744 (Baptism, **St. Werburgh Parish**)

Peter Ussher (father):

Residence - Hoyes Alley - December 10, 1737

  November 12, 1739

  October 26, 1741

  December 1742

  January 15, 1744

  September 20, 1745

- Peter Ussher & Elizabeth Craig

  - Thomas Ussher – b. 5 Dec 1863, bapt. 30 Dec 1863 (Baptism, **St. Michan Parish (RC)**)

  - Monica Ussher – b. 1865, bapt. 1865 (Baptism, **St. Andrew Parish (RC)**)

  - Margaret Ussher – b. 23 Jun 1868, bapt. 6 Jul 1868 (Baptism, **St. Michan Parish (RC)**)

Peter Ussher (father):

Residence - 131 Upper Dorset Street - December 30, 1863

  5 Marks Street - 1865

  Cody Lane - July 6, 1868

Hurst

- Peter Ussher, bur. 6 Jan 1728 (Burial, **St. Peter Parish**) & Elizabeth Unknown

  - George Ussher – bapt. 7 Nov 1714 (Baptism, **St. Peter Parish**)

  - Martha Ussher – bapt. 15 Jan 1715 (Baptism, **St. Peter Parish**)

  - Thomas Ussher – bur. 3 Feb 1717 (Burial, **St. Peter Parish**)

  - Elizabeth Ussher – bapt. 28 Jul 1717 (Baptism, **St. Peter Parish**), bur. 22 Aug 1717 (Burial, **St. Peter Parish**)

  - Frances Ussher – bapt. 20 Oct 1718 (Baptism, **St. Peter Parish**), bur. 6 Nov 1718 (Burial, **St. Peter Parish**)

  - Margaret Ussher – bapt. 4 Feb 1721 (Baptism, **St. Peter Parish**)

  - John Ussher – bapt. 20 Jan 1722 (Baptism, **St. Peter Parish**), bur. 28 Feb 1722 (Burial, **St. Peter Parish**)

Peter Ussher (father):

Residence - King Street - February 3, 1717

July 28, 1717

August 22, 1717

February 4, 1721

February 28, 1722

- Peter Ussher & Judith Unknown

  - Peter Ussher – bapt. 1818 (Baptism, **St. Andrew Parish** (RC))

- Peter Ussher & Mary Byrne (B y r n e)

  - Peter Ussher – b. 4 Aug 1878, bapt. 11 Aug 1878 (Baptism, **St. Joseph Parish** (RC))

Peter Ussher (father):

Residence - Upper Kimmage - August 11, 1878

Ussher Surname Ireland: 1600s to 1900s

- Richard Ussher & Catherine Bryan

  o Jane Ussher – b. 19 Oct 1807, bapt. 19 Oct 1807 (Baptism, **Causeway Parish** (RC))

Richard Ussher (father):

Residence - Kilmore - October 19, 1807

- Richard Ussher & Catherine Stack

  o Mary Ussher – b. 28 Aug 1891, bapt. 30 Aug 1891 (Baptism, **Causeway Parish** (RC))

  o Catherine Ussher – b. 28 Apr 1894, bapt. 3 May 1894 (Baptism, **Causeway Parish** (RC))

  o Richard Ussher – b. 4 Jun 1895, bapt. 8 Jun 1895 (Baptism, **Causeway Parish** (RC))

  o Elizabeth Ussher – b. 16 Mar 1900, bapt. 18 Mar 1900 (Baptism, **Causeway Parish** (RC))

Richard Ussher (father):

Residence - Ardoughter - August 30, 1891

May 3, 1894

June 8, 1895

March 18, 1900

- Richard Ussher & Elizabeth Ussher

  o Sarah Ussher – bapt. 30 Jan 1778 (Baptism, **St. Luke Parish**)

  o Noble Luke Sheldon Ussher, bapt. 21 Jan 1781 (Baptism, **St. Luke Parish**) & Mary Ussher

    ▪ William Ussher – bapt. 3 Jan 1808 (Baptism, **St. Mary Parish**)

    ▪ Francis Warren Ussher – bapt. 20 Feb 1809 (Baptism, **St. Mary Parish**)

  o George Ussher – bapt. 1 Apr 1782 (Baptism, **St. Luke Parish**)

Richard Ussher (father):

Residence - Coombe - January 30, 1778

January 21, 1781

April 1, 1782

Occupation - Apothecary - January 30, 1778

January 21, 1781

April 1, 1782

Hurst

- Richard Ussher & Elizabeth Ussher

  - Dorothea Ussher – bapt. 24 Apr 1786 (Baptism, **St. Mary Parish**)

  - Elizabeth Ussher – bapt. 9 May 1787 (Baptism, **St. Mary Parish**)

- Richard Ussher & Ellen Danehy – 29 Jan 1814 (Marriage, **Cork - South Parish** (RC))

  - Honora Ussher – bapt. 16 Nov 1817 (Baptism, **Cork - South Parish** (RC))

  - Margaret Ussher – bapt. 29 Sep 1828 (Baptism, **Cork - South Parish** (RC))

Ellen Denahy (mother):

Residence - 3 Hatch Lane - January 29, 1814

- Richard Ussher & Jane Kennelly

  - William Ussher – b. 5 Jun 1825, bapt. 5 Jun 1825 (Baptism, **Listowel Parish** (RC))

  - Honora Ussher – b. 13 May 1832, bapt. 13 May 1832 (Baptism, **Moyvane Parish** (RC))

Richard Ussher (father):

Residence - Moyvane - June 5, 1825

Clounbrane - May 13, 1832

- Richard Ussher & Mary Hussey – 25 May 1819 (Marriage, **Causeway Parish** (RC))

  - Mary Ussher – b. 15 Dec 1821, bapt. 15 Dec 1821 (Baptism, **Causeway Parish** (RC))

  - Honora Ussher – b. 3 Jul 1824, bapt. 3 Jul 1824 (Baptism, **Causeway Parish** (RC))

  - Margaret Ussher – b. 20 Apr 1827, bapt. 20 Apr 1827 (Baptism, **Causeway Parish** (RC))

  - Michael Ussher – b. 13 Oct 1838, bapt. 13 Oct 1838 (Baptism, **Causeway Parish** (RC))

Richard Ussher (father):

Residence - Paddoch - May 25, 1819

Gralig - December 15, 1821

April 20, 1827

Meenogahane - July 3, 1824

Mary Hussey (mother):

Residence - Paddoch - May 25, 1819

Ussher Surname Ireland: 1600s to 1900s

- Richard Ussher & Unknown

    o Richard John Ussher & Elizabeth Owen Finlay – 20 Jan 1866 (Marriage, **Clondalkin Parish**)

        ▪ Arthur Hamilton Ussher – b. 1869, bapt. 1869 (Baptism, **Clondalkin Parish**)

        ▪ Neville Osbourne Ussher – b. 1873, bapt. 1873 (Baptism, **Clondalkin Parish**)

Richard John Ussher (son):

Residence - Cappagh, Cappoquin, Co. Waterford - January 20, 1866

Cappagh, Co. Waterford - 1869

1873

Occupation - Gentleman - January 20, 1866

1873

J. P. (Probably abbreviated for Justice of the Peace) 1869

Elizabeth Owen Finlay, daughter of John William Finlay (daughter-in-law):

Residence - Corkagh, Clondalkin - January 20, 1866

Occupation - Lady - January 20, 1866

John William Finlay (father):

Occupation - Clergyman

Richard Ussher (father):

Occupation - Gentleman

- Robert Ussher & Bridget Tevington

    o Elizabeth Anne Ussher – b. 31 Apr 1857, bapt. 8 May 1857 (Baptism, **St. Mary, Pro Cathedral Parish (RC)**)

Robert Ussher (father):

Residence - Kingstown - May 8, 1857

- Robert Ussher & Helen Coppinger – 21 Feb 1816 (Marriage, **St. Mary Parish**)

    o Thomas Henry Ussher – bapt. 27 Nov 1817 (Baptism, **St. Michan Parish (RC)**)

- Robert Ussher & Helen Unknown

    o Robert Ussher – bapt. 1829 (Baptism, **St. Andrew Parish (RC)**)

- Robert Ussher & Honora Kissane

  o John Ussher – b. 3 Jul 1839, bapt. 3 Jul 1839 (Baptism, **Causeway Parish (RC)**)

Robert Ussher (father):

Residence - Kilmore - July 3, 1839

- Robert Ussher & Jane Ussher

  o Theophilus Ussher – bapt. 10 Jan 1637 (Baptism, **St. Michan Parish**)

  o Margaret Ussher – bapt. 29 Jun 1639 (Baptism, **St. Michan Parish**)

  o Marks Ussher – bapt. 9 Oct 1640 (Baptism, **St. Michan Parish**)

Robert Ussher (father):

Occupation - Lo. Bishop of Kildare - January 10, 1637

June 29, 1639

October 9, 1640

Professional Title - Dr.

- Robert Ussher & Jane Ussher

  o Elizabeth Ussher – b. 23 Apr 1847, bapt. 9 Jun 1847 (Baptism, **St. George Parish**)

Robert Ussher (father):

Residence - 157 Great Britain Street - June 9, 1847

Occupation - Basket Maker - June 9, 1847

- Robert Ussher & Mary Staunton – 2 Jul 1817 (Marriage, **St. George Parish**) (Marriage, **St. Mary, Pro Cathedral Parish** (RC))

  o Robert Ussher – bapt. 3 May 1818 (Baptism, **St. Mary Parish**)

  o Richard John Ussher – bapt. 17 Oct 1822 (Baptism, **St. Mary, Pro Cathedral Parish** (RC))

Robert Ussher (father):

Residence - Abbey Street - July 2, 1817

Occupation - Esquire - July 2, 1817

Ussher Surname Ireland: 1600s to 1900s

- Robert Ussher & Mary Sturdy

  o Richard Ussher – b. 25 Oct 1833, bapt. 25 Oct 1833 (Baptism, **Causeway Parish (RC)**)

Robert Ussher (father):

Residence - Kilmore - October 25, 1833

- Robert Ussher & Unknown

  o Anne Ussher & Henry Harden – 5 Feb 1853 (Marriage, **St. Thomas Parish**)

Signatures:

Anne Ussher (daughter):

Residence - 48 Lower Buckingham Street- February 5, 1853

Henry Harden, son of George Harden (son-in-law):

Residence - 12 Castleview Terrace, Co. Cork - February 5, 1853

Occupation - Engineer - February 5, 1853

Henry Harden (father):

Occupation - Gentleman

Robert Ussher (father):

Occupation - Gentleman

Wedding Witnesses:

Thomas Sparks & William Harden

Signatures:

Hurst

- o Helen Ussher & William Lings Victor – 17 Apr 1856 (Marriage, **St. Thomas Parish**)

Helen Ussher (daughter):

Residence - 48 Lower Buckingham Street - April 17, 1856

William Lings Victor, son of John George Victor (son-in-law):

Residence - Dundalk - April 17, 1856

Occupation - Gentleman - April 17, 1856

John George Victor (father):

Occupation - Lieutenant Royal Navy

Robert Ussher (father):

Occupation - Gentleman

- Robert Ussher & Unknown

  - o William Ussher & Susan Simpson Reilly – 12 Jun 1861 (Marriage, **St. Mary Parish**)

Signatures:

William Ussher (son):

Residence - 52 Upper Dorset Street - June 12, 1861

Occupation - Gentleman - June 12, 1861

Relationship Status at Marriage - widow

Susan Simpson, daughter of Alexander Simpson (daughter-in-law):

Residence - 52 Upper Dorset Street - June 12, 1861

Relationship Status at Marriage - widow

Ussher Surname Ireland: 1600s to 1900s

Alexander Simpson (father):

Occupation - Glover

Robert Ussher (father):

Occupation - Merchant

- Thomas Ussher & Bridget Fitzgerald – 2 Nov 1802 (Marriage, **Cork - South Parish (RC)**)

  o Thomas Ussher – bapt. 3 Nov 1809 (Baptism, **Cork - SS. Peter & Paul Parish (RC)**)

  o Thomas Ussher – bapt. 13 Mar 1811 (Baptism, **Cork - SS. Peter & Paul Parish (RC)**)

Thomas Ussher (father):

Residence - Christ Church Lane - November 2, 1802

Cockpit Lane - November 3, 1809

March 13, 1811

Bridget Fitzgerald (mother);

Residence - Fish Street - November 2, 1802

- Thomas Ussher & Caroline Warren – 14 Nov 1810 (Marriage, **St. Peter Parish**)

- Thomas Ussher & Catherine Unknown

  o Noble Luke Ussher – b. 21 Jul 1815, bapt. 9 Aug 1815 (Baptism, **St. Peter Parish**)

- Thomas Ussher & Elizabeth Unknown

  o Elizabeth Ussher – bapt. 17 Aug 1743 (Baptism, **St. Catherine Parish**)

- Thomas Ussher & Elizabeth Ussher

  o Thomas Ussher – bapt. 22 Jun 1827 (Baptism, **St. Mary, Pro Cathedral Parish (RC)**)

  o Thomas Ussher – bapt. 2 Jan 1831 (Baptism, **St. Mary, Pro Cathedral Parish (RC)**)

Thomas Ussher (father):

Residence - Sackville Lane - June 22, 1827

Hurst

- Thomas Ussher & Elizabeth Wallace

  - Monica Mary Ussher – b. 6 Sep 1856, bapt. 8 Sep 1856 (Baptism, **St. Michan Parish (RC)**)

Thomas Ussher (father):

Residence - 72 Dominick Street - September 8, 1856

- Thomas Ussher & Elizabeth Jane Ussher

  - Thomas Ussher – b. 7 Apr 1827, bapt. 29 Apr 1827 (Baptism, **St. Mary Parish**)

  - Edward Ussher – bapt. 29 Mar 1829 (Baptism, **St. Mary Parish**)

  - James Ussher – bapt. 6 Sep 1835 (Baptism, **St. Mary Parish**)

Thomas Ussher (father):

Residence - 2 Sackville Court - March 29, 1829

        13 Upper Liffey Street - September 6, 1835

Occupation - Mat Maker - March 29, 1829

        Rope Mat Maker - September 6, 1835

- Thomas Ussher & Euphemia Sophia Unknown

  - William Percival Ussher – b. 20 Aug 1838, bapt. 2 Sep 1838 (Baptism, **St. Werburgh Parish**)

Signatures:

o   Sophia Louisa Ussher & James Pickthall – 21 Apr 1862 (Marriage, **St. Mark Parish**)

Signatures:

Sophia Louisa Ussher (daughter):

   Residence - 2 George's Street George's Quay - April 21, 1862

James Pickthall, son of Thomas Pickthall (son-in-law):

   Residence - 2 George's Street George's Quay - April 21, 1862

   Occupation - Mariner - April 21, 1862

Thomas Pickthall (father);

   Occupation - Gentleman

Thomas Ussher (father):

   Occupation - Gentleman

Wedding Witnesses:

William Percival Ussher & David Campbell

Signatures:

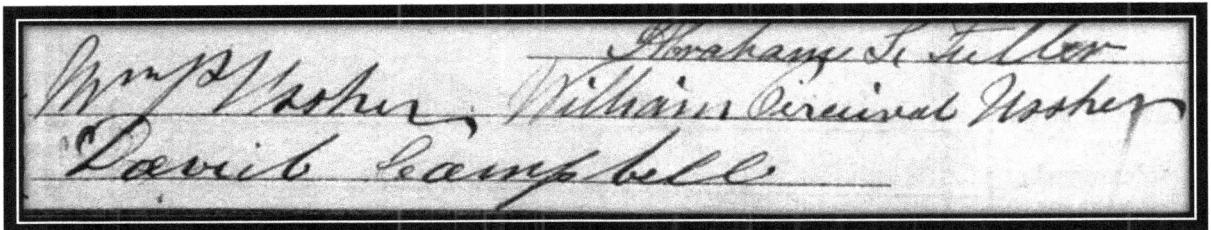

- o Alice Richards Ussher & George Connor – 8 Jan 1869 (Marriage, **St. Mark Parish**)

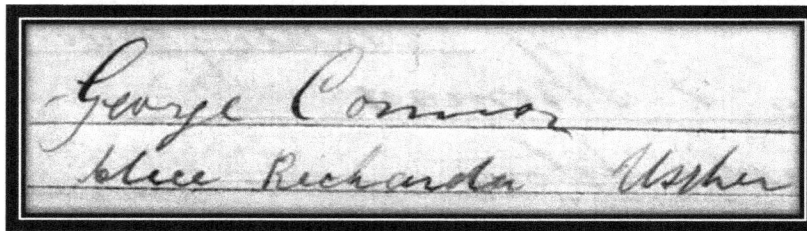

Signatures:

Alice Richards Ussher (daughter):

    Residence - 34 Deuzille Street - January 8, 1869

George Connor, son of George Connor (son-in-law):

    Residence - 34 Deuzille Street - January 8, 1869

    Occupation - Laborer - January 8, 1869

George Connor (father):

    Occupation - Baker

Thomas Ussher (father);

    Occupation - Gentleman

Wedding Witnesses:

Robert Smith & William Percival Ussher

Signatures:

Ussher Surname Ireland: 1600s to 1900s

- Thomas Ussher & Frances Unknown
  - Thomas Ussher – bapt. 4 Oct 1743 (Baptism, **St. Catherine Parish**)

- Thomas Ussher & Genita Unknown
  - James Ussher – bapt. 1763 (Baptism, **St. Andrew Parish (RC)**)

- Thomas Ussher & Guphunia Unknown
  - Rebecca Mary Ussher – bapt. 4 Dec 1840 (Baptism, **St. Nicholas Within Parish**)

Thomas Ussher (father):

Residence - 57 Back Lane - December 4, 1840

Occupation - Writing Clerk - December 4, 1840

- Thomas Ussher & Honora Church – 6 Feb 1835 (Marriage, **Causeway Parish (RC)**)

Thomas Ussher (husband):

Residence - Ratoo - February 6, 1835

- Thomas Ussher & Honora Driscoll
  - Jasper Ussher – b. 16 Mar 1826. bapt. 16 Mar 1826 (Baptism, **Causeway Parish (RC)**)

Thomas Ussher (The Father):

Residence - Kilmore - March 16, 1826

- Thomas Ussher & Honora Regan – 4 Feb 1889 (Baptism, **Causeway Parish (RC)**)
  - Edward Ussher – b. 1 Nov 1889, bapt. 3 Nov 1889 (Baptism, **Causeway Parish (RC)**)
  - Ellen Ussher – b. 18 Feb 1895, bapt. 23 Feb 1895 (Baptism, **Causeway Parish (RC)**)
  - Elizabeth Ussher – b. 5 Aug 1896, bapt. 8 Aug 1896 (Baptism, **Causeway Parish (RC)**)
  - Michael Ussher – b. 14 Sep 1898, bapt. 17 Sep 1898 (Baptism, **Causeway Parish (RC)**)
  - Thomas Ussher – b. 20 Aug 1899, bapt. 26 Aug 1899 (Baptism, **Causeway Parish (RC)**)

Hurst

Thomas Ussher (father):

Residence - Ballyduff - February 4, 1889

Kilmore - November 3, 1889

Clahane - February 23, 1895

August 8, 1896

September 17, 1898

August 26, 1899

Honora Regan (mother):

Residence - Ballyduff - February 4, 1889

- Thomas Ussher & Jane Ussher

  o James Ussher – bapt. 15 Sep 1835 (Baptism, **St. Mary, Pro Cathedral Parish** (RC))

- Thomas Ussher & Mary Kelly

  o Mary Anne Ussher – bapt. 1893 (Baptism, **St. Andrew Parish** (RC))

Thoms Ussher (father):

Residence - 182 Townsend Street - 1893

- Thomas Ussher & Mary McSweeney

  o Edward Ussher – b. 19 Aug 1834, bapt. 19 Aug 1834 (Baptism, **Causeway Parish** (RC))

Thomas Ussher (father):

Residence - Kilmore - August 19, 1834

- Thomas Ussher & Mary Ryan – 20 Jul 1823 (Marriage, **St. Andrew Parish** (RC))

  o Joseph Ussher – bapt. 1824 (Baptism, **St. Andrew Parish** (RC))

  o John Ussher – bapt. 1826 (Baptism, **St. Andrew Parish** (RC))

- Thomas Ussher & Mary Anne Butler – 1 Feb 1853 (Marriage, **St. Mary, Pro Cathedral Parish** (RC))

  o William Joseph Ussher – bapt. 30 Nov 1853 (Baptism, **St. Michan Parish** (RC))

- Thomas Ussher & Mary Anne Unknown

  o Richard Ussher – bapt. 4 Jun 1819 (Baptism, **St. Peter Parish**)

Ussher Surname Ireland: 1600s to 1900s

- Thomas Ussher & Mary Anne Unknown

  o Thomas F. Ussher – bapt. 1828 (Baptism, **St. Andrew Parish (RC)**)

- Thomas Ussher & Monica Ryan – 17 Nov 1833 (Marriage, **St. Mary, Pro Cathedral Parish (RC)**)

  o Peter Ussher – bapt. 26 Jun 1835 (Baptism, **St. Mary, Pro Cathedral Parish (RC)**)

- Thomas Ussher & Rebecca Durham

  o Rebecca Mary Ussher – b. 19 Dec 1862, bapt. 12 Oct 1881 (Baptism, **St. Mary, Pro Cathedral Parish (RC)**)

Thomas Ussher (father):

Residence - 110 Great Britain Street - October 12, 1881

- Thomas Ussher & Rose Unknown

  o Stephen Ussher –bapt. 25 May 1838 (Baptism, **St. Mary, Pro Cathedral Parish (RC)**)

- Thomas Ussher & Sophia Ussher

  o Frances Lucinda Ussher – b. 13 Jul 1851, bapt. 24 Feb 1852 (Baptism, **St. Peter Parish**)

Thomas Ussher (father):

Residence - 1 New Bride Street - February 24, 1852

Occupation - Shop Keeper - February 24, 1852

- Thomas Ussher & Sophia Ussher

  o John George Samuel Ussher – b. 13 Dec 1854, bapt. 14 Jun 1864 (Baptism, **St. Mark Parish**)

Thomas Ussher (father):

Residence - 2 East George's Street - June 14, 1864

Occupation - House Holder - June 14, 1864

Hurst

- Thomas Ussher & Unknown

  - Robert Ussher & Mary Abigail Fox – 8 Dec 1864 (Marriage, **St. Peter Parish**)

Signatures:

Robert Ussher (son):

    Residence - 30 Mount Pleasant Avenue - December 8, 1864

    Occupation - Gentleman - December 8, 1864

Mary Abigail Fox, daughter of William Smyth Fox (daughter-in-law):

    Residence - Lucan - December 8, 1864

William Smyth Fox (father):

Signature:

    Occupation - Clerk in Holy Orders

Thomas Ussher (father):

    Occupation - Surgeon

Wedding Witnesses:

Allan N. Fox & William Smyth Fox

Signatures:

- Thomas Ussher & Unknown

  o Fanny Ussher & Robert Hill – 2 Dec 1874 (Marriage, **St. Mary Parish**)

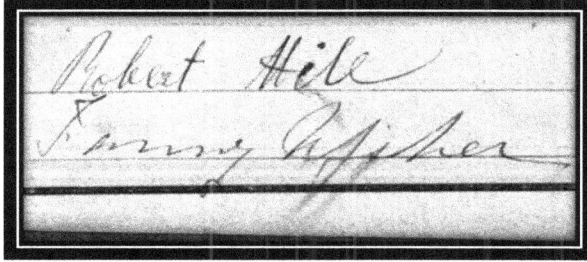

Signatures:

Fanny Ussher (daughter);

   Residence - 102 Dorset Street Upper - December 2, 1874

Robert Hill, son of Abraham Hill (son-in-law):

   Residence - 102 Dorset Street Upper - December 2, 1874

   Occupation - Gas Fitter - December 2, 1874

Abraham Hill (father):

   Occupation - Mariner

Thoms Ussher (father):

   Occupation - Mercantile Clerk

- Thomas Ussher & Unknown

  - Robert Ussher & Mary Anne Allen – 15 Feb 1887 (Marriage, **Milltown Parish**)

Signatures:

Robert Ussher (son):

    Residence - Boyne View Brogheda - February 15, 1887

    Occupation - Esquire - February 15, 1887

Mary Anne Allen, daughter of Joseph Allen (daughter-in-law):

    Residence - 16 Belgrave Square - February 15, 1887

Joseph Allen (father):

Signature:

    Occupation - Merchant

Thomas Ussher (father):

    Occupation - Land Agent

Wedding Witnesses:

Joseph Allen & Francis J. Ussher

Signatures:

Ussher Surname Ireland: 1600s to 1900s

- Thomas Ussher & Unknown

  o Charles Ussher & Mary O'Brien Keable – 24 Nov 1893 (Marriage, **St. Stephen Parish**)

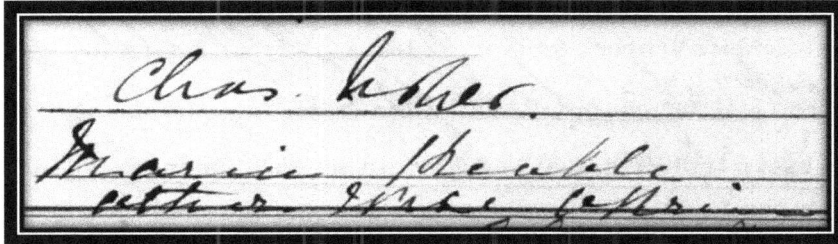

Signatures:

Charles Ussher (son):

  Residence - Beggars Bush Barracks - November 24, 1893

  Occupation - Sergeant Drummer Sussex Regiment - November 24, 1893

Mary O'Brien Keable, daughter of Bernard O'Brien (daughter-in-law):

  Residence - 115 Haddington Road, Dublin - November 24, 1893

  Relationship Status at Marriage - widow

Bernard O'Brien (father):

  Occupation - Esquire

Thomas Ussher (father):

  Occupation - Soldier

- Timothy Ussher & Margaret Unknown

  o Francis Ussher – bapt. 1827 (Baptism, **St. Andrew Parish (RC)**)

- Unknown Ussher & Margaret Bradford

  o Caroline Mary Ussher – b. 1874, bapt. 1874 (Baptism, **St. Andrew Parish (RC)**)

Unknown Ussher (father):

  Residence - 4 Stephen's Place - 1874

- Unknown Ussher & Unknown

  o St. Lawrence Ussher – bapt. 6 Sep 1747 (Baptism, **St. Michan Parish (RC)**)

Hurst

- Unknown Ussher & Unknown

  o Jane Mary Ussher – b. 3 Jan 1859, bapt. 4 Jan 1859 (Baptism, **St. Audoen Parish (RC)**)

Unknown Ussher (father):

Residence - Usher's Street - January 4, 1859

- Unknown Ussher & Unknown

  o Stephen Ussher – b. 1878, bapt. 28 Nov 1878 (Baptism, **St. Audoen Parish (RC)**)

Unknown Ussher (father):

Residence - 10 Usher's Quay - November 28, 1878

- Unknown Ussher & Unknown

  o Elizabeth Cooper Ussher & Hermann (H e r m a n n) Linderer – 25 Aug 1886 (Marriage, **St. Peter Parish**)

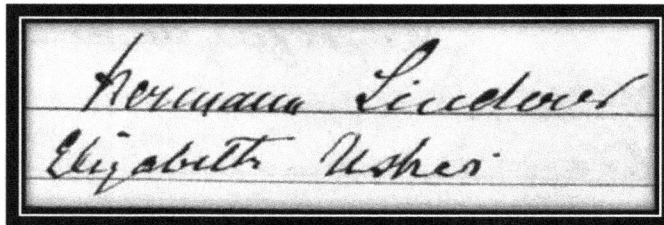

Signatures:

Elizabeth Ussher (daughter):

Residence - Blue Coat School & Abbeyleix - August 25, 1886

Relationship Status at Marriage - widow

Hermann Linderer, son of Joseph Charles Linderer (son-in-law):

Residence - The Molyneux Asylum Leeson Park - August 25, 1886

Occupation - Caretaker - August 25, 1886

Relationship Status at Marriage - widow

Ussher Surname Ireland: 1600s to 1900s

Joseph Charles Linderer (father):

Occupation - M D

Robert Cooper (father):

Occupation - Cabinet Maker

- Walter Ussher & Unknown

  o Mary Ussher – bur. 25 Jan 1621 (Burial, **St. John Parish**)

- Westly Ussher & Mary Ussher

  o John Ussher – bapt. 10 Jul 1804 (Baptism, **St. Mark Parish**)

Westly Ussher (father):

Residence - Townsend Street - July 10, 1804

- William Ussher & Anne Mary Ussher

  o Jane Isabel Catherine Ussher – b. 7 Nov 1872, bapt. 28 Nov 1872 (Baptism, **St. Peter Parish**)

William Ussher (father):

Residence - 4 Cluttenham Place - November 28, 1872

Occupation - Clerk - November 28, 1872

- William Ussher & Elizabeth Unknown

  o Mary Anne Ussher – bapt. 13 Oct 1766 (Baptism, **St. Werburgh Parish**)

William Ussher (father):

Residence - Darby's Square - October 13, 1813

Hurst

- William Ussher & Elizabeth Jane Unknown

  o Mary Elizabeth Ussher – b. 6 Nov 1885, bapt. 3 Jan 1886 (Baptism, **St. Catherine Parish**)

  o Thomas Ussher – b. 28 Mar 1891, bapt. 29 Mar 1891 (Baptism, **St. Mark Parish**)

  o Christina Margaret Ussher – b. 15 Apr 1893, bapt. 7 May 1893 (Baptism, **St. Mark Parish**)

  o Elizabeth Jane Ussher – b. 22 Jan 1894, bapt. 17 Feb 1895 (Baptism, **St. Mark Parish**)

  o Henry George Ussher – b. 10 Jun 1898, bapt. 3Jul 1898 (Baptism, **St. Mark Parish**)

William Ussher (father):

Residence - 14 Braithwaite Street - January 3, 1886

5 Sandwith Place - March 29, 1891

May 7, 1893

3 Sandwith Place - February 17, 1895

July 3, 1898

Occupation - Van-Man - January 3, 1886

July 3, 1898

Van Driver - March 29, 1891

May 7, 1893

February 17, 1894

- William Ussher & Frances Ussher

  o Violet Wilhelmina Ussher – b. 6 Feb 1897, bapt. 25 Feb 1897 (Baptism, **St. George Parish**)

William Ussher (father):

Residence - 49 Mountjoy Square - February 25, 1897

Occupation - Gardener - February 25, 1897

Ussher Surname Ireland: 1600s to 1900s

- William Ussher & Frances Alicia Ussher

  o Anne Ussher – bapt. 20 Dec 1835 (Baptism, **St. Mary Parish**)

  o Benjamin Hamilton Ussher – b. 2 Jun 1838, bapt. 29 Jun 1838 (Baptism, **St. Mary Parish**)

  o William Ussher – b. 5 Jun 1841, bapt. 27 Jun 1841 (Baptism, **St. George Parish**)

  o Frances Alicia Ussher – b. 1 Jul 1843, bapt. 6 Aug 1843 (Baptism, **St. Mary Parish**)

  o Alicia Ussher – b. 24 Nov 1844, bapt. 16 Mar 1845 (Baptism, **St. Mary Parish**)

William Ussher (father):

Residence - 2 Middle Mountjoy Street - December 20, 1835

June 29, 1838

Langford Terrace Royal Canal - June 27, 1841

23 Lower Ormond Quay - August 6, 1843

25 Lower Ormond Quay - March 16, 1845

Occupation - Coach Maker - December 20, 1835

June 27, 1841

August 6, 1843

March 16, 1846

Private Gentleman - June 29, 1838

- William Ussher & Hannah Mary Ussher

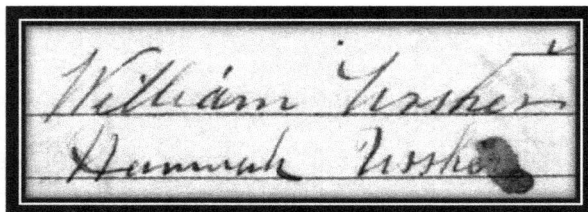

- o Charles William Ussher – b. 28 Apr 1862, bapt. 30 May 1862 (Baptism, **St. Mark Parish**)

- o Thomas Henry Ussher – b. 27 Jul 1864, bapt. 4 Sep 1864 (Baptism, **St. Mark Parish**)

- o John James Ussher – b. 11 Mar 1867, bapt. 31 Mar 1867 (Baptism, **Irishtown Parish**)

- o Samuel Edward Ussher – b. 4 Aug 1871, bapt. 20 Aug 1871 (Baptism, **Irishtown Parish**)

William Ussher (father):

Residence - 2 East George's Street - May 30, 1862

September 4, 1864

5 Bath Avenue - March 31, 1867

24 Bath Avenue - August 20, 1871

Occupation - Printer - May 30, 1862

September 4, 1864

August 20, 1871

Boot Maker - March 31, 1867

- William Ussher & Jane Martin

- o Elizabeth Ussher – bapt. 18 Jan 1842 (Baptism, **St. Catherine Parish (RC)**)

Ussher Surname Ireland: 1600s to 1900s

- William Ussher, bur. 22 Jan 1718 (Burial, **St. Audoen Parish**) & Leticia Mary Ussher, bur. 15 Nov 1732 (Burial, **St. Audoen Parish**)

  o Martha Ussher – bapt. 25 Jun 1696 (Baptism, **St. Audoen Parish**), bur. 1 May 1709 (Burial, **St. Audoen Parish**)

  o Leticia Ussher – bapt. 20 Jun 1697 (Baptism, **St. Audoen Parish**), bur. 12 Oct 1701 (Burial, **St. Audoen Parish**)

  o Xpher Ussher – bapt. 9 Jul 1698 (Baptism, **St. Audoen Parish**)

  o Christopher Ussher – bur. 8 Apr 1699 (Burial, **St. Audoen Parish**)

  o William Ussher – bapt. 21 Aug 1703 (Baptism, **St. Audoen Parish**)

  o Henry Ussher – bapt. 24 Sep 1706 (Baptism, **St. Audoen Parish**)

  o Leticia Ussher – bapt. 19 Jan 1707 (Baptism, **St. Audoen Parish**), bur. 13 Aug 1713 (Burial, **St. Audoen Parish**)

  o Martha Ussher – bapt. 27 Jul 1712 (Baptism, **St. Audoen Parish**)

William Ussher (father):

Occupation - Esquire - April 8, 1699

> **October 12, 1701**
> **August 21, 1703**
> **September 24, 1706**
> **January 19, 1707**
> **July 27, 1712**

- William Ussher & Mary Peppard

  o Lucy Ussher – b. 1899, bapt. 1899 (Baptism, **St. Andrew Parish (RC)**)

William Ussher (father):

Residence - Holles Street Hospital - 1899

- William Ussher & Mary Pepper

  o Matthew Ussher – b. 1889, bapt. 1889 (Baptism, **St. Andrew Parish** (RC))

William Ussher (father):

Residence - 3 Harmony Row - 1889

- William Ussher & Mary Unknown

  o John Ussher – bur. 25 Sep 1774 (Burial, **St. Luke Parish**)

John Ussher (son):

Residence - Coombe - September 25, 1774

Cause of Death - small pox

- William Ussher & Mary Unknown

  o Mary Anne Ussher – bapt. 23 Jul 1775 (Baptism, **St. Michan Parish** (RC))

- William Ussher & Mary Unknown

  o William John Ussher – b. 20 Sep 1839, bapt. 20 Oct 1839 (Baptism, **St. Peter Parish**)

William Ussher (father):

Residence - Pembroke Street - October 20, 1839

- William Ussher & Mary Unknown

  o Mary Ussher – b. 28 Jun 1884, bapt. 21 Jun 1888 (Baptism, **St. Stephen Parish**)

  o Thomas Ussher – b. 27 May 1887, bapt. 21 Jun 1888 (Baptism, **St. Stephen Parish**)

William Ussher (father):

Residence - 7 Grant's Row - June 21, 1888

Occupation - Laborer - June 21, 1888

- William Ussher & Mary Anne Unknown

  o Mary Ussher – b. 1895, bapt. 1896 (Baptism, **St. Andrew Parish** (RC))

William Ussher (father):

Residence - 118 Townsend Street - 1896

Ussher Surname Ireland: 1600s to 1900s

- William Ussher & Mary Ussher

  o Sarah Ussher – bapt. 25 Mar 1723 (Baptism, **St. Catherine Parish**)

- William Ussher & Mary Ussher

  o John Ussher – bapt. 12 Apr 1725 (Baptism, **St. Luke Parish**)

  o Thomas Ussher – bapt. 25 May 1737 (Baptism, **St. Luke Parish**)

  o William Ussher – bapt. 17 Dec 1744 (Baptism, **St. Luke Parish**)

- William Ussher & Mary Ussher

  o James Ussher – bapt. 23 Sep 1738 (Baptism, **St. Catherine Parish**)

  o Catherine Ussher – bapt. 4 Nov 1739 (Baptism, **St. Catherine Parish**)

  o Thomas Ussher – bapt. 17 Jan 1740 (Baptism, **St. Catherine Parish**)

- William Ussher & Sarah Ussher

  o Henry Ussher – bur. 27 Oct 1723 (Burial, **St. Mary Parish**)

- William Ussher & Unknown

  o John Ussher – bur. 9 Sep 1713 (Burial, **St. Audoen Parish**)

Hurst

- William Ussher & Unknown

  - Charles Ussher, b. 1837 & Isabel Cooper, b. 1837 – 3 Apr 1861 (Marriage, **Grangegorman Parish**)

Signatures:

Charles Ussher (son):

    Residence - No 1 Norton's Row Phibsborough - April 3, 1861

    Occupation - Office Clerk - April 3, 1861

Isabel Cooper, daughter of Robert Cooper (daughter-in-law):

    Residence - No 1 Norton's Phibsborough

    Occupation - Millianor - April 3, 1861

Robert Cooper (father):

    Occupation - Cabnatorn Maker

William Ussher (father):

    Occupation - Clerk

Wedding Witnesses:

Patrick Greene & Jane Cooper

Signatures:

- William Ussher & Unknown

  - Nannie Ussher & John McCleery – 2 Nov 1858 (Marriage, **St. George Parish**)

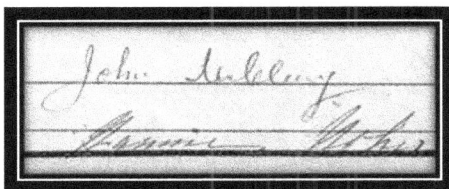

Signatures:

Nannie Ussher (daughter):

    Residence - 16 Grenville Street & Dundalk - November 2, 1858

John McCleery, son of Hugh McCleery (son-in-law):

    Residence - Francis Street Dundalk -November 2, 1858

    Occupation - Commercial Clerk - November 2, 1858

Hugh McCleery (father):

    Occupation - Esquire

William Ussher (father):

    Occupation - Esquire

Wedding Witnesses:

William Woods & Robert McCleery

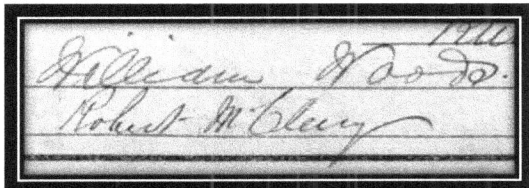

Signatures:

- Whistly Ussher & Mary Unknown

  - Mary Ussher – bapt. 1793 (Baptism, **St. Andrew Parish (RC)**)

- Xpher Ussher & Martha Ussher

  - Martha Ussher – bapt. 17 Jul 1677 (Burial, **St. Audoen Parish**)

  - Florence Ussher – bur. 3 Oct 1682 (Burial, **St. Audoen Parish**)

Individual Births/Baptisms

- Elizabeth Ussher – bapt. 10 Jun 1834 (Baptism, **St. Audoen Parish**)

- Henrietta Ussher – b. 23 Mar 1766, bapt. Unclear (Baptism, **St. Paul Parish**)

- Henry Ussher – bapt. 20 Mar 1720 (Baptism, **St. Patrick Parish**)

- Thomas Ussher – bapt. 20 Mar 1720 (Baptism, **St. Patrick Parish**)

Individual Burials

- Ada Ussher – b. Jun 1867, bur. 6 Nov 1869 (Burial, **St. George Parish**)

Ada Ussher (deceased):

    Residence - Lower Dorset Street - Before November 6, 1869

    Age at Death - 2 ½ years

- Adam Ussher – bur. 26 May 1713 (Burial, **St. Paul Parish**)

- Adam Ussher – bur. 10 Sep 1745 (Burial, **St. Audoen Parish**)

Adam Ussher (deceased):

    Residence - Clontarf - Before September 10, 1745

- Alice Ussher – bur. 14 Oct 1625 (Burial, **St. John Parish**)

- Anne Ussher – bur. 28 Jun 1650 (Burial, **St. John Parish**)

- Anne Ussher – bur. 16 Oct 1729 (Burial, **St. Audoen Parish**)

- Arthur Ussher – bur. 24 Nov 1707 (Burial, **St. Audoen Parish**)

Arthur Ussher (deceased):

    Occupation - Esquire - November 24, 1707

- Barbara Ussher (Mrs.) – bur. 15 Mar 1745 (Burial, **St. Patrick Parish**)

- Bell Ussher – bur. 19 Sep 1782 (Burial, **St. Mark Parish**)

- Caroline Ussher – b. 1789, bur. 13 Sep 1816 (Burial, **St. Peter Parish**)

- Caroline Rosanna Ussher – b. 1833, bur. 25 Dec 1836 (Burial, **St. Peter Parish**)

Caroline Rosanna Ussher (deceased):

    Residence - South Wing Street - Before December 25, 1836

    Age at Death - 3 years

    Place of Burial - St. Peter's Cemetery

- Catherine Ussher – bur. 22 Jan 1740 (Burial, **St. Catherine Parish**)

- Charles Ussher (Child) – bur. 27 Jun 1727 (Burial, **St. Catherine Parish**)

- Charles Ussher – bur. 2 Jan 1770 (Burial, **St. Audoen Parish**)

Charles Ussher (deceased):

    Residence - Caple Street - Before January 2, 1770

    Occupation - Esquire - January 2, 1770

- Christian Elizabeth Ussher – b. Jul 1820, bur. 9 Oct 1820 (Burial, **St. Peter Parish**)

Christian Elizabeth Ussher (deceased):

    Residence - Digges Street - Before October 9, 1820

    Age at Death - 4 months

    Place of Burial - St. Kevin's Churchyard

- Christiana E. Ussher – b. 1800, bur. 12 Jun 1870 (Burial, **St. George Parish**)

Christiana E. Ussher (deceased):

    Residence - 19 Richmond Cottages - Before June 12, 1870

- Christopher Ussher – bur. 27 Mar 1742 (Burial, **St. Mary Parish**)

- Christopher Ussher – bur. 5 Sep 1763 (Burial, **St. Audoen Parish**)

Christopher Ussher (deceased):

    Occupation - Esquire - September 5, 1763

- Daniel Ussher – bur. 2 Jan 1740 (Burial, **St. Catherine Parish**)

- Eleanor Ussher – bur. 4 Oct 1690 (Burial, **St. John Parish**)

- Elizabeth Ussher (Mrs.) – bur. 31 Jan 1706 (Burial, **St. Catherine Parish**)

- Elizabeth Ussher – b. 1650, bur. 2 Apr 1718 (Burial, **St. Werburgh Parish**)

Elizabeth Ussher (deceased):

    Residence - Blind Key - Before April 2, 1718

    Cause of Death - age

- Elizabeth Ussher – bur. 27 Jul 1725 (Burial, **St. Audoen Parish**)

Ussher Surname Ireland: 1600s to 1900s

- Elizabeth Ussher – bur. 28 Mar 1787 (Burial, **St. Catherine Parish**)

Elizabeth Ussher (deceased):

> **Residence - Alms House - Before March 28, 1787**

- Elizabeth Ussher – bur. 22 Feb 1824 (Burial, **Clontarf Parish**)

- Elizabeth Ussher – b. 1742, bur. 28 Dec 1826 (Burial, **Clontarf Parish**)

Elizabeth Ussher (deceased):

> **Age at Death - 84 years**

- Emma Ussher – b. 1824, bur. 11 Dec 1889 (Burial, **Taney Parish**)

Emma Ussher (deceased):

> **Residence - Kingstown - Before December 11, 1889**
>
> **Age at Death - 65 years**

- Esme Ussher – bur. 11 Feb 1715 (Burial, **St. Paul Parish**)

- Esther Ussher – b. 1852, bur. 18 Apr 1857 (Burial, **St. Audoen Parish**)

Esther Ussher (deceased):

> **Age at Death - infant**
>
> **Remarks (Birth) - foundling**

- Frances Ussher – bur. 11 Dec 1738 (Burial, **St. Audoen Parish**)

Frances Ussher (deceased):

> **Residence - Mouldsworth Street - Before December 11, 1738**

- Frances Ussher – b. 1835, bur. 29 Dec 1836 (Burial, **St. Catherine Parish**)

Frances Ussher (deceased):

> **Residence - Meath Street - Before December 29, 1836**
>
> **Age at Death - 1 ¼ years**

- George Ussher (Child) – bur. 25 Sep 1721 (Burial, **St. Catherine Parish**)

- George Ussher – bur. 7 May 1734 (Burial, **St. Peter Parish**)

Hurst

- Henrietta Fanny Jane Ussher – b. Feb 1827, bur. 9 Aug 1828 (Burial, **Clontarf Parish**)

Henrietta Fanny Jane Ussher (deceased):

> **Age at Death - 18 months**

- Henry Ussher – bur. 11 Feb 1729 (Burial, **St. Mary Parish**)

- Henry Ussher – bur. 6 Dec 1741 (Burial, **St. Audoen Parish**)

Henry Ussher (deceased):

> **Residence - Usher's Quay - Before December 6, 1741**

- Henry Ussher – bur. 23 Jan 1761 (Burial, **St. Audoen Parish**)

Henry Ussher (deceased):

> **Residence - King Street, Stephen's Green - Before January 23, 1761**

- James Ussher – bur. 28 Jan 1665 (Burial, **St. John Parish**)

James Ussher (deceased):

> **Occupation - Soldier - January 28, 1665**

- James Ussher – bur. 18 Jul 1740 (Burial, **St. Mary Parish**)

- James Ussher (Child) – bur. 13 May 1743 (Burial, **St. Mary Parish**)

- Jane Ussher – bur. 22 Feb 1824 (Burial, **Clontarf Parish**)

- Jane Ussher – bur. Aug 1701 (Burial, **St. Nicholas Without Parish**)

Jane Ussher (deceased):

> **Residence - Frans Street - Before August 1701**

- Jane Ussher – bur. 23 April Unclear (Burial, **St. Luke Parish**)

- John Ussher – bur. 25 Jun 1648 (Burial, **St. John Parish**)

- John Ussher – bur. 2 Aug 1650 (Burial, **St. John Parish**)

- John Ussher – bur. 17 Jun 1739 (Burial, **St. Paul Parish**)

John Ussher (deceased):

> **Professional Title - Dr.**

- John Ussher – bur. 9 Dec 1794 (Burial, **St. Paul Parish**)

Ussher Surname Ireland: 1600s to 1900s

- John Ussher – bur. 15 Oct 1810 (Burial, **St. Peter Parish**)

John Ussher (deceased):

    Residence - Harcourt Street - Before October 15, 1810

- John Ussher – b. 1815, bur. 25 Jun 1824 (Burial, **St. Mark Parish**)

- John Ussher – b. 1822, d. 21 Mar 1825, bur. 1825 (Burial, **St. Peter Parish**)

John Ussher (deceased):

    Residence - Marlborough Street - March 21, 1825

    Age at Death - 3 years

- John Ussher – b. Aug 1831, bur. 6 Feb 1832 (Burial, **Clontarf Parish**)

John Ussher (deceased):

    Residence - Black Rock, Co. Dublin - Before February 6, 1832

    Age at Death - 6 months

- John Ussher – b. May 1870, bur. 18 Jul 1870 (Burial, **Irishtown Parish**)

John Ussher (deceased):

    Residence - Dahlia Terrace - Before July 18, 1870

    Age at Death - 2 months

- Joseph Ussher – bur. 10 Jan 1777 (Burial, **St. James Parish**)

Joseph Ussher (deceased):

    Residence - King Street - Before January 10, 1777

- Leticia Ussher – bur. 24 Oct 1729 (Burial, **St. Audoen Parish**)

- Leticia Ussher – b. 1815, bur. 1 Nov 1847 (Burial, **St. Luke Parish**)

Leticia Ussher (deceased):

    Residence - Cork Street Hospital - Before November 1, 1847

- Margaret Ussher – bur. 22 Aug 1798 (Burial, **St. Peter Parish**)

Margaret Ussher (deceased):

    Residence - Stephen Street - Before August 22, 1798

Hurst

- Margaret Ussher – b. 1797, bur. 30 Jan 1837 (Burial, **St. Mark Parish**)

Margaret Ussher (deceased):

Residence - Sir John's Quay - Before January 30, 1837

- Marks Ussher – bur. 6 Jun 1742 (Burial, **St. Paul Parish**)

- Mary Ussher – bur. 21 Oct 1732 (Burial, **St. Catherine Parish**)

- Mary Ussher – bur. 21 Aug 1773 (Burial, **St. Michael Parish**)

Mary Ussher (deceased):

Residence - Dawson Street - Before August 21, 1773

- Mary Ussher – b. 1819, bur. 4 Jul 1834 (Burial, **St. Peter Parish**)

Mary Ussher (deceased):

Residence - Digges Lane - Before July 4, 1834

Age at Death - 15 years

Place of Burial - St. Kevin Cemetery

- Nicholas Ussher – bur. 5 Dec 1769 (Burial, **St. James Parish**)

Nicholas Ussher (deceased):

Residence - John Jerusalem - Before December 5, 1769

- Ralph Ussher – bur. 19 Sep 1782 (Burial, **St. Mark Parish**)

- Robert Ussher – bur. 30 Dec 1642 (Burial, **St. John Parish**)

- Sarah Ussher – bur. 29 Dec 1737 (Burial, **St. Mary Parish**)

- Thomas Ussher – b. 1753, bur. 22 Aug 1823 (Burial, **St. Mary Parish**)

Thomas Ussher (deceased):

Residence - Sackville Lane - Before August 22, 1823

- Thomas Ussher – b. 1827, bur. 20 Jun 1833 (Burial, **St. Peter Parish**)

Thomas Ussher (deceased):

Residence - 6 Lower Rutland Street - Before June 20, 1833

Age at Death - 6 years

Place of Burial - St. Peter Cemetery

Ussher Surname Ireland: 1600s to 1900s

- Thomas Ussher – b. 1778, bur. 1 Mar 1858 (Burial, **St. Peter Parish**)

Thomas Ussher (deceased):

    Residence - 2 Home Ville, Rathmines - Before March 1, 1858

    Age at Death - 80 years

- Unknown Ussher – bur. 11 Mar 1720 (Burial, **St. Nicholas Without Parish**)

Unknown Ussher (deceased):

    Residence - New Street - Before March 11, 1720

- Unknown Ussher – bur. 18 Feb 1743 (Burial, **St. Audoen Parish**)

Unknown Ussher (deceased):

    Occupation - Arch-Deacon - February 18, 1743

- Unknown Ussher – bur. 8 Jul 1747 (Burial, **St. Audoen Parish**)

Unknown Ussher (deceased):

    Occupation - Esquire - July 8, 1747

- Unknown Ussher (Male Child) – bur. 18 Mar 1762 (Burial, **St. Mary Parish**)

Unknown Ussher (deceased):

    Residence - St. George's - Before March 18, 1762

- Unknown Ussher – bur. 6 Sep 1764 (Burial, **St. Audoen Parish**)

Unknown Ussher (deceased):

    Residence - Mount Ussher, Co. Wicklow - Before September 6, 1764

- Unknown Ussher – bur. 24 May 1775 (Burial, **St. James Parish**)

Unknown Ussher (deceased):

    Residence - Chanel Row - Before May 24, 1775

- Unknown Ussher – bur. 21 Feb 1801 (Burial, **St. Mary Parish**)

Unknown Ussher (deceased):

    Residence - Abbey Street - Before February 21, 1801

- Unknown Ussher, Miss – bur. 26 Apr 1745 (Burial, **St. Mary Parish**)

- Unknown Ussher, Miss – b. 1831, bur. 19 Sep 1831 (Burial, **Clontarf Parish**)

Unknown Ussher, Miss (deceased):

    Residence - Dublin - Before September 19, 1831

    Age at Death - 3 weeks

    Remarks - Miss Ussher Great Granddaughter of the late Rev. Dr. Ussher

- Unknown Ussher, Mr. – bur. 10 Nov 1796 (Burial, **St. Mary Parish**)

Unknown Ussher, Mr. (deceased):

    Residence - Strand Street - Before November 10, 1796

- Unknown Ussher, Mr. – bur. 30 Jun 1806 (Burial, **St. Mary Parish**)

Unknown Ussher, Mr. (deceased):

    Residence - Abbey Street - Before June 30, 1806

- Unknown Ussher, Mrs. – bur. 23 Aug 1748 (Burial, **St. Audoen Parish**)

Unknown Ussher, Mrs. (deceased):

    Residence - Jervis Street - Before August 23, 1748

- Unknown Ussher, Mrs. – bur. 10 Mar 1764 (Burial, **St. Audoen Parish**)

Unknown Ussher, Mrs. (deceased):

    Residence - Clare Street - Before March 10, 1764

- Unknown Ussher, Mrs. – bur. 29 Oct 1803 (Burial, **St. Mary Parish**)

Unknown Ussher, Mrs. (deceased):

    Residence - Mecklenburgh Street - Before October 29, 1803

- Unknown Ussher, Mrs. – bur. 17 Jul 1803 (Burial, **St. Audoen Parish**)

Unknown Ussher, Mrs. (deceased):

    Residence - Stephen's Green - Before July 17, 1764

- Violet W. Ussher – b. Feb 1897, bur. 22 Oct 1898 (Burial, **St. George Parish**)

Violet W. Ussher (deceased):

    Residence - 9 George's Place - Before October 22, 1898

Ussher Surname Ireland: 1600s to 1900s

- Walter Ussher – bur. 7 Apr 1636 (Burial, **St. John Parish**)

Walter Ussher (deceased):

   Occupation - Alderman - April 7, 1636

- Walter Ussher – bur. 15 Dec 1698 (Burial, **St. Catherine Parish**)

- William Ussher – bur. 11 Jun 1643 (Burial, **St. John Parish**)

- William Ussher – bur. 18 Mar 1686 (Burial, **St. Michan Parish**)

William Ussher (deceased):

   Occupation - Esquire - March 18, 1686

   Relationship Status at Death - bachelor

- William Ussher – bur. 14 Mar 1704 (Burial, **St. Audoen Parish**)

- William Ussher – bur. 30 Jul 1707 (Burial, **St. Catherine Parish**)

- William Ussher (Child) – bur. 30 May 1725 (Burial, **St. Catherine Parish**)

- William Ussher – bur. 16 Mar 1764 (Burial, **St. James Parish**)

William Ussher (deceased):

   Residence - Earl Street - Before March 16, 1764

- William Ussher – bur. 18 Mar 1807 (Burial, **St. James Parish**)

William Ussher (deceased):

   Residence - Marlborough Street - Before March 18, 1807

- William Ussher – b. 1782, bur. 17 May 1817 (Burial, **St. Peter Parish**)

- William Ussher – b. 1830, bur. 10 Mar 1835 (Burial, **St. Mark Parish**)

William Ussher (deceased):

   Residence - Townsend Street - Before March 10, 1835

   Age at Death - 5 years

Individual Marriages

- Ales Ussher & William Barry – 1 Nov 1678 (Marriage, **St. Audoen Parish**)

- Anne Ussher & George H. Dunne – 13 Aug 1873 (Marriage, **St. Mary, Haddington Road Parish** (RC))

- Anne Ussher & Patrick Byrne (B y r n e) – 26 Feb 1811 (Marriage, **St. Andrew Parish** (RC))

- Anne Ussher & Thaddeus Sullivan

  o Mary Sullivan – b. 20 Jun 1807, bapt. 20 Jun 1807 (Baptism, **Tralee Parish** (RC))

Thaddeus Sullivan (father):

Residence - Causeway - June 20, 1807

- Anne Ussher & Walter Connor – 19 Dec 1782 (Marriage, **St. Nicholas Parish** (RC))

- Arrabella Ussher & Charles Edward Molloy – 6 Mar 1810 (Marriage, **St. Peter Parish**)

- Barbara Ussher & John Byrne (B y r n e) – 10 May 1818 (Marriage, **St. Michan Parish** (RC))

- Bridget Ussher & Edward Connor

  o Edward Connor – b. 26 Nov 1885, bapt. 29 Nov 1885 (Baptism, **Causeway Parish** (RC))

Edward Connor (father):

Residence - Kilmore - November 29, 1885

- Bridget Ussher & John Gallagher

  o Esther Gallagher – bapt. 7 Jul 1776 (Baptism, **St. Nicholas Parish** (RC))

- Bridget Ussher & John Gavagan – 8 Nov 1807 (Marriage, **St. Mary, Pro Cathedral Parish** (RC))

Ussher Surname Ireland: 1600s to 1900s

- Bridget Ussher & Michael Mahony

  o Dermot (D e r m o t) Mahony – b. 25 May 1837, bapt. 25 May 1837 (Baptism, **Causeway Parish (RC)**)

Michael Mahony (father):
Residence - Kilmore - May 25, 1837

- Bridget Ussher & Patrick Reilly – 17 Jan 1785 (Marriage, **St. Catherine Parish (RC)**)

- Catherine Ussher & Edward Quinn

  o Mary Quinn – bapt. 11 Dec 1768 (Baptism, **St. Nicholas Parish (RC)**)

- Catherine Ussher & James Caulfield – 12 Feb 1774 (Marriage, **St. Nicholas Parish (RC)**)

- Catherine Ussher & James Walsh – 27 Aug 1835 (Marriage, **Ballylongford Parish (RC)**)

  o Michael Walsh – b. 1 Nov 1839, bapt. 1 Nov 1839 (Baptism, **Ballylongford Parish (RC)**)

Catherine Ussher (mother):
Residence - Tieraclea - August 27, 1835

James Walsh (father):
Residence - Tieraclea - November 1, 1839

- Catherine Ussher & John Dignum

  o Thomas Dignum – bapt. 1774 (Baptism, **SS. Michael & John Parish (RC)**)

- Catherine Ussher & Michael O'Shaughnessy

  o Robert O'Shaughnessy – b. 1860, bapt. 1861 (Baptism, **St. Andrew Parish (RC)**)

Michael O'Shaughnessy (father):
Residence - Grattan Place - 1861

- Catherine Ussher & Richard Gaffney

  o Mary Gaffney – bapt. Apr 1816 (Baptism, **St. Nicholas Parish (RC)**)

  o Elizabeth Gaffney – bapt. 5 Oct 1828 (Baptism, **St. Nicholas Parish (RC)**)

- Catherine Ussher & Richard Sparks – 22 Oct 1793 (Marriage, **St. Bride Parish**)

Richard Sparks (husband):

Occupation - Gentleman - October 22, 1793

- Eleanor Ussher & John Brassier – 13 Sep 1760 (Marriage, **St. Michan Parish (RC)**)

- Eleanor Usher & John Ferguson – 28 Sep 1748 (Marriage, **St. Michan Parish**)

John Ferguson (husband):

Occupation - Esquire - September 28, 1748

- Elizabeth Ussher & Henry Shannahan

  o   Anne Shannahan – bapt. 1 Jul 1815 (Baptism, **Cork - South Parish (RC)**)

- Elizabeth Ussher & James Carroll – 8 Jul 1637 (Marriage, **St. John Parish**)

- Elizabeth Ussher & James Colclough – 15 Apr 1827 (Marriage, **St. Michan Parish (RC)**)

- Elizabeth Ussher & James Mayfield

  o   Dominick Mayfield – bapt. 31 Jan 1779 (Baptism, **St. James Parish (RC)**)

  o   Mary Mayfield – bapt. 13 Jun 1781 (Baptism, **St. James Parish (RC)**)

- Elizabeth Ussher & John Anderson – 30 Apr 1790 (Marriage, **St. Mary Parish**)

John Anderson (husband):

Residence - Co. Dublin - April 30, 1790

Occupation - Calico Printer - April 30, 1790

- Elizabeth Ussher & Matthew Madden – 12 Feb 1811 (Marriage, **SS. Michael & John Parish (RC)**)

  o   Edward Madden – bapt. 19 Jan 1812 (Baptism, **SS. Michael & John Parish (RC)**)

  o   Mary Anne Madden – bapt. 27 Feb 1814 (Baptism, **SS. Michael & John Parish (RC)**)

  o   Joan Madden – bapt. 31 Aug 1817 (Baptism, **St. Nicholas Parish (RC)**)

Wedding Witnesses:

Robert Ussher

Ussher Surname Ireland: 1600s to 1900s

- Elizabeth Ussher & Michael Ryan

  o Michael St. John Ryan – bapt. 1849 (Baptism, **St. Mary, Haddington Road Parish (RC)**)

- Elizabeth Ussher & Timothy Finn

  o Elizabeth Mary Finn – b. 29 Apr 1897, bapt. 1 May 1897 (Baptism, **St. Mary, Pro Cathedral Parish (RC)**)

  o Sarah Finn – b. 3 Aug 1898, bapt. 5 Aug 1898 (Baptism, **St. Mary, Pro Cathedral Parish (RC)**)

Timothy Finn (father):

Residence - 71 Great Britain Street - May 1, 1897

August 5, 1898

- Elizabeth Ussher & William Langrill

  o Harriet Langrill – bapt. 1871 (Baptism, **St. Andrew Parish (RC)**)

William Langrill (father):

Residence - 55 York Street - 1871

- Elizabeth Anne Ussher & John Rowan – 26 Mar 1780 (Marriage, **St. Anne Parish**)

John Rowan (husband):

Occupation - Esquire - March 26, 1780

- Ellen Ussher & John Brenan

  o James Brenan – bapt. 27 Jan 1803 (Baptism, **Cork - South Parish (RC)**)

John Brenan (father):

Residence - Gillabby Cross - January 27, 1803

- Ellen Ussher & Patrick Carroll

  o Margaret Carroll – b. 24 Jul 1809, bapt. 24 Jul 1809 (Baptism, **Causeway Parish (RC)**)

Patrick Carroll (father):

Residence - Clashmalcan East - July 24, 1809

Hurst

- Ellen Ussher & Thomas Stundan

  o Mary Stundan – b. 10 May 1813, bapt. 10 May 1813 (Baptism, **Causeway Parish** (RC))

  o Ellen Stundan – b. 4 Jan 1824, bapt. 4 Jan 1824 (Baptism, **Causeway Parish** (RC))

Thomas Stundan (father):

Residence - Kilmore - May 10, 1813

January 4, 1824

- Ellis Ussher & Kavennis Blake – 25 Oct 1817 (Marriage, **St. Peter Parish**)

Kavennis Blake (husband):

Residence - Oranmore, Co. Galway - October 25, 1817

Wedding Witness:

Christopher Ussher

- Emily Ussher & John Harman (H a r m a n)

  o Emily Harman (H a r m a n) – b. 3 Jun 1884, bapt. 13 Jun 1884 (Baptism, **St. Mary, Pro Cathedral Parish** (RC))

John Harman (father):

Residence - 40 Upper Mecklinburgh Street - June 13, 1884

- Emily Ussher & William Wayland

  o George Wayland – bapt. 26 Aug 1853 (Baptism, **St. Mary, Pro Cathedral Parish** (RC))

  o Robert Wayland – bapt. 26 Aug 1853 (Baptism, **St. Mary, Pro Cathedral Parish** (RC))

  o William Wayland – bapt. 26 Aug 1853 (Baptism, **St. Mary, Pro Cathedral Parish** (RC))

William Wayland (father):

Residence - 38 Buckingham Street - August 26, 1853

Ussher Surname Ireland: 1600s to 1900s

- Esther Ussher & Cornelius (C o r n e l i u s) Devlin

    o Joseph Devlin – b. 8 Jul 1874, bapt. 20 Jul 1874 (Baptism, **St. Michan Parish (RC)**)

    o Mary Anne Devlin – b. 17 Sep 1879, bapt. 26 Sep 1879 (Baptism, **St. Nicholas Parish (RC)**)

Cornelius Devlin (father):

Residence - 67 Mary's Lane - July 20, 1874

42 Golden Lane - September 26, 1879

- Esther Ussher & Patrick Murray

    o Elizabeth Murray – bapt. 24 Dec 1783 (Baptism, **St. Catherine Parish (RC)**)

- Frances Ussher & Patrick Latin – 29 Jun 1827 (Marriage, **St. Andrew Parish (RC)**)

    o Mark Latin – bapt. 25 Jul 1834 (Baptism, **St. Nicholas Parish (RC)**)

- Frances Ussher & William Neville

    o Eily Elizabeth Mary Neville – b. 6 Apr 1884, bapt. 16 Apr 1884 (Baptism, **St. Mary, Pro Cathedral Parish (RC)**)

William Neville (father):

Residence - 12 Upper Gloster Street - April 16, 1884

- Hannah Ussher & Daniel Brown – 12 Jan 1717 (Marriage, **St. John Parish**)

- Hannah Ussher & Michael Moran

    o Bridget Moran – bapt. 24 Jun 1804 (Baptism, **St. Catherine Parish (RC)**)

- Honor Ussher & James Ryan

    o James Ryan – b. 18 Nov 1835, bapt. 18 Nov 1835 (Baptism, **Causeway Parish (RC)**)

James Ryan (father):

Residence - Kilmore - November 18, 1835

- Jane Ussher & Gulielmo Paul

    o Patrick Paul – bapt. 1828 (Baptism, **St. Nicholas Parish (RC)**)

Hurst

- Jane Ussher & Michael Connan – 22 Nov 1840 (Marriage, **St. Mary, Pro Cathedral Parish** (RC))

- Judith Ussher & Robert Taylor – 13 Dec 1696 (Marriage, **St. Audoen Parish**)

Robert Taylor (husband):

Occupation - Esquire - December 13, 1696

- Lucy Ussher & John Patchell

  o Mary Patchell – bapt. 1890 (Baptism, **St. Andrew Parish** (RC))

John Patchell (father):

Residence - 2 Albert Court - 1890

- Margaret Ussher & Bryan Rogers – 18 Jun 1763 (Marriage, **St. Catherine Parish** (RC))

  o Anne Rogers – bapt. 30 Aug 1769 (Baptism, **St. Catherine Parish** (RC))

  o Sarah Rogers – bapt. 18 Nov 1770 (Baptism, **St. Catherine Parish** (RC))

  o Hugh Rogers – bapt. 14 Jul 1780 (Baptism, **St. Catherine Parish** (RC))

  o Bryan Rogers – bapt. 23 Nov 1783 (Baptism, **St. Catherine Parish** (RC))

- Margaret Ussher & Matthew Conroy – 19 Jun 1717 (Marriage, **St. Andrew Parish** (RC))

- Margaret Ussher & Patrick Brookes – 12 Apr 1807 (Marriage, **St. Andrew Parish** (RC))

- Margaret Ussher & Paul Kearns (K e a r n s) – 25 Sep 1783 (Marriage, **St. Catherine Parish** (RC))

- Martha Ussher & Anthony Marley – 26 Oct 1740 (Marriage, **St. Audoen Parish**)

Anthony Marley (husband):

Occupation - Esquire - October 26, 1740

- Martha Ussher & Cornelius (C o r n e l i u s) Spain

  o Henrietta Elizabeth Spain – bBapt. Jun 1814 (Baptism, **St. Nicholas Parish** (RC))

- Martha Ussher & Nehemiah Danilan – 21 Mar 1693 (Marriage, **St. Audoen Parish**)

Nehemiah Danilan (husband):

Occupation - Esquire - March 21, 1693

Ussher Surname Ireland: 1600s to 1900s

- Mary Ussher & Alexander McDaniel

  - Nancy McDaniel – bapt. 10 May 1798 (Baptism, **Cork - SS. Peter & Paul Parish (RC)**)

Alexander McDaniel (father):

Residence - North Mayo - May 10, 1798

- Mary Ussher & Bigse Henzeyard – 22 Jul 1735 (Marriage, **St. Peter Parish**)

- Mary Ussher & Charles Farrell

  - Thomas Farrell – b. 20 Sep 1892, bapt. 25 Sep 1892 (Baptism, **Causeway Parish (RC)**)

  - Catherine Farrell – b. 21 Oct 1894, bapt. 1 Nov 1894 (Baptism, **Causeway Parish (RC)**)

  - Mary Farrell – b. 7 Nov 1896, bapt. 16 Nov 1896 (Baptism, **Causeway Parish (RC)**)

  - Elizabeth Farrell – b. 9 Mar 1899, bapt. 12 Mar 1899 (Baptism, **Causeway Parish (RC)**)

  - James Farrell – b. 3 Dec 1900, bapt. 8 Dec 1900 (Baptism, **Causeway Parish (RC)**)

Charles Farrell (father):

Residence - Cashen - September 25, 1892

November 16, 1896

Kilmore - November 1, 1894

March 12, 1899

Clahane - December 8, 1900

- Mary Ussher & Christopher Blake

  - Ellen Blake – bapt. 29 May 1843 (Baptism, **St. Nicholas Parish (RC)**)

- Mary Ussher & Christopher McDonagh

  - Catherine McDonagh – bapt. 3 Aug 1819 (Baptism, **St. Michan Parish (RC)**)

- Mary Ussher & John Congrave – 29 Apr 1758 (Marriage, **St. Anne Parish**)

John Congrave (husband):

Occupation - Esquire - April 29, 1758

Hurst

- Mary Ussher & John Patrick Moore

    o Unknown Moore – b. 18 May 1844, bapt. 18 May 1844 (Baptism, **Causeway Parish** (RC))

    o Jane Moore – b. 25 May 1847, bapt. 25 May 1847 (Baptism, **Causeway Parish** (RC))

John Moore (father):

Residence - Meenogahane - May 18, 1844

May 25, 1847

- Mary Ussher & Joseph Doyle – 14 Jul 1754 (Marriage, **St. Catherine Parish** (RC))

- Mary Ussher & Isaac Eades

    o Mary Eades – bapt. 17 Apr 1846 (Baptism, **St. Michan Parish** (RC))

    o Mary Anne Eades – bapt. 26 Mar 1849 (Baptism, **St. Michan Parish** (RC))

- Mary Ussher & Michael Kirwan

    o William Thomas Kirwan – b. 3 Oct 1896, bapt. 5 Oct 1896 (Baptism, **St. Mary, Pro Cathedral Parish** (RC))

Michael Kirwan (father):

Residence - 147 Upper Abbey Street - October 5, 1896

- Mary Ussher & Patrick Long

    o Jane Long & Thomas Conroy – 24 Jul 1859 (Marriage, **St. Nicholas Parish** (RC))

Jane Long (daughter):

Residence - 52 New Row - July 24, 1859

Thomas Conroy, son of Peter Conroy & Bridget Reilly (son-in-law):

Residence - 52 New Row - July 24, 1859

- Mary Ussher & Richard Baldwin – 7 Oct 1734 (Marriage, **St. Bride Parish**)

Richard Baldwin (husband):

Occupation - Esquire - October 7, 1734

Ussher Surname Ireland: 1600s to 1900s

- Mary Ussher & Thomas Andrews – 26 Jun 1779 (Marriage, **St. Mary Parish**)

Thomas Andrews (husband):

Residence - Drogheda - June 26, 1779

- Mary Anne Ussher & Gulielmo Henry Vance – 8 Nov 1855 (Marriage, **St. Nicholas Parish** (RC))

- Rebecca Ussher & John Stone

  o Rebecca Margaret Stone – b. 1894, bapt. 1895 (Baptism, **St. Andrew Parish** (RC))

  o Michael Joseph Stone – b. 26 Mar 1897, bapt. 19 Apr 1897 (Baptism, **SS. Michael & John Parish**

  (RC))

John Stone (father):

Residence - 12 Cuffe Street - 1895

         26 Digges Street - April 19, 1897

- Sarah Ussher & James Cranfield – 22 Nov 1799 (Marriage, **St. Mary Parish**)

James Cranfield (husband):

Professional Title - Rev.

Name Variations

Includes Latin and Abbreviated forms of names found in the original documents.

Abigail = Abigale, Abigall

Anne = Ann, Anna, Annae

Bartholomew = Barth, Bartholmeus, Bartholomeo

Benjamin = Benj

Bridget = Birgis, Brigid, Brigida, Bridgit

Catherine = Catharine, Catharina, Catharinae, Catherina, Cath, Catha, Cathae, Cathe, Cathn, Kate

Charles = Carolus, Charls, Chas

Christopher = Christoph

Daniel = Danielem, Danielis

Edward = Ed, Edwd, Edmund, Edmond

Eleanor = Eleo, Eleonora, Elinor, Ellenor

Elizabeth = Betty, Elisa, Elisabeth, Eliz, Eliza, Elizab, Elizh, Elizth

Ellen = Elena, Ellena

Esther = Essie, Ester

Francis = Fransicum

George = Geo, Georg, Georgius

Grace = Gratiae

Gulielmo = Guil, Guillelmi, Gulielmum, Guillelmus, Gulmi

Harold = Harry

Honora = Hanora

Ussher Surname Ireland: 1600s to 1900s

Hugh = Hew

James = Jacobi, Jacobus, Jas

Jane = Joanna

Jeanne = Jeannae, Joannae

Joan = Johanna, Joney

John = Jno, Joannem, Joannes, Johannis

Joseph = Jos

Leticia = Letitia, Lettice, Letticia

Lewis = Louis

Luke = Lucas

Margaret = Margarita, Margaritae, Margeret, Marget, Margt

Martha = Marthae

Mary = Maria, My

Mary Anne = Marianna, Marianne, Maryanne

Michael = Michaelis, Michl

Patrick = Pat, Patt, Patk, Patricii, Patricius

Peter = Petri

Ralph = Ralfe

Richard = Ricardi, Ricardus, Rich, Richd

Robert = Roberti

Rose = Rosa, Rosae

Samuel = Samuelis

Thomas = Thom, Thomae, Thoms, Thos, Ths

Timothy = Timotheus, Timy

Valentine = Val, Valentinae, Valentinus

William = Wil, Will, Willm, Wm

Notes

Notes

Notes

Notes

Hurst

Notes

Notes

$\mathfrak{I}$ndex

D

Ussher Surname Ireland: 1600s to 1900s

Ussher Surname Ireland: 1600s to 1900s

Hurst

Hurst

About The Author

Donovan Hurst graduated from San Diego State University with a Bachelor of Arts in the major field of studies of History and a minor in the field of studies of Anthropology. He is a current member of The General Society of Mayflower Descendants and has been conducting genealogical research for over 10 years tracing back his ancestors to their ancestral homelands in Denmark, England, France, Germany, Ireland, Norway, and Scotland.